Training Your Pug

Brenda Belmonte

D1449931

BARRON'S

About the Author

Brenda Belmonte's love of dogs began over 20 years ago. She continues to participate with multiple breeds in both conformation and obedience dog shows throughout the United States. She is a Judges Educational Instructor for the Pug Dog Club of America, a Canine Good Citizen evaluator for the American Kennel Club, and an experienced all-breed obedience instructor. Brenda owns a dog training business in Illinois and has been the practice manager for a veterinary clinic for over 20 years. She specializes in behavior and nutrition, and provides guidance and behavioral services to new puppy owners. She is a breed columnist for the *AKC Gazette* and *Pug Talk Magazine*. Brenda is also the author of *The Pug Handbook* and *The Silky Terrier Manual*, both published by Barron's Educational Series.

All inquiries should be addressed to:
Barron's Educational Series, Inc.
250 Wireless Boulevard
Hauppauge, NY 11788
www.barronseduc.com

ISBN-13: 978-0-7641-4029-7
ISBN-10: 0-7641-4029-9

Library of Congress Catalog Card No. 2008016937

Library of Congress Cataloging-in-Publication Data
Belmonte, Brenda.
    Training your pug / Brenda Belmonte.
        p. cm.
    Includes index.
    ISBN-13: 978-0-7641-4029-7
    ISBN-10: 0-7641-4029-9
    1. Pug — Training. I. Title.

SF429.P9B453   2008
636.76—dc22   2008016937

Printed in China
9 8 7 6 5 4 3 2 1

Acknowledgments

This book is dedicated to all of the individuals that have had the courage to train and compete with their Pugs. Each Pug that graduates from a training course or qualifies for its "leg's" in obedience or "Q"s in Agility proves that with a little bit of patience, some perseverance, and a good sense of humor, you can successfully train a Pug.

Cover Credits

Front and back covers: Shutterstock; inside front cover: Cheryl Ertelt; inside back cover: Pets by Paulette.

Photo Credits

Cheryl Ertelt: 9, 43, 51, 62, and 130; Jean Fogle: 86, 89, 107, 108, 127, 133, and 142; Isabelle Francais: 8, 14, 21, 24, 34, 41, 58, 59, 64, 66, 68, 69, 78, 104, 111, 112, 135, 137, 143, and 144; Pets by Paulette: 2, 5, 6, 7, 11, 15, 17, 18, 19, 20, 22, 25, 27, 28, 29, 30, 31, 35, 36, 37, 40, 42, 46, 49, 50, 53, 61, 63, 65, 72, 77, 81, 84, 91, 94, 97, 100, 103, 114, 128, 140, 146, and 147; Connie Summers/Paulette Johnson: 12, 32, 60, 79, 82, 85, 88, 118, and 124.

A Word About Pronouns

Many dog lovers feel that the pronoun "it" is not appropriate when referring to a pet that can be such a wonderful part of our lives. For this reason, Pugs are described as "he" or "she" in alternating chapters throughout this book. This by no means infers any preference, nor should it be taken as an indication that either sex is particularly problematic.

Important Note

This book tells the reader how to train a Pug. The author and the publisher consider it important to point out that the advice given in the book is meant primarily for dogs of excellent physical health and good character.

Anyone who adopts a fully grown dog should be aware that the animal has already formed its basic impressions of human beings. There are dogs that as a result of bad experiences with humans behave in an unnatural manner or may even bite. Only people that have experience with dogs should take in such an animal.

Even well-behaved and carefully supervised dogs sometimes do damage to someone else's property or cause accidents. It is, therefore, in the owner's interest to be adequately insured against such eventualities, and we strongly urge all dog owners to purchase a liability policy that covers their dog.

Contents

1 *Introduction*

For decades, the Pug has been blessed with a wonderful reputation. Pugs make perfect companions for individuals of any age, families on the go, and have been a popular choice for movie stars, sports celebrities, and those of royal bloodlines. Pug lovers will tell you that there is no other breed like it!

Why Train Your Pug?

When the decision is made to add a dog to a household, very few people intentionally allow the dog to become out of control, destructive, or a bully. It is unfortunate that all too often people are poorly prepared to take the necessary steps to properly train and socialize their new canine addition. Animal shelters are full of dogs that were discarded by their owners for behavior problems and rescue groups from coast to coast have Pugs waiting to be re-homed.

While the Pug is small in size, one that is out-of-control can spell trouble and cause endless frustration. You should be willing to learn about your Pug's behavior and be committed to making him a well-behaved canine citizen before problems arise. By

dedicating the necessary time, energy, and effort to teaching your Pug what you want him to do, and preventing him from learning bad behaviors, you will find that a Pug can make a terrific companion. But in order to train your Pug you will need to learn about normal dog behaviors, understand how dogs communicate, and know how these relate to your Pug.

Normal Canine Behaviors

All domestic dogs share a distant common ancestor: the wolf. The behaviors of wolves have been thoroughly studied and documented, with many books and movies available to learn about their social hierarchy, behavior patterns, and communication skills. While early domestication and the subsequent selective breeding by man produced dogs that vary widely in size, shape, and appearance, many of the behaviors attributed to the dog's wild origin remain apparent even today. Dogs have a complex way of interacting within their own social group. The behaviors that are associated with normal canine interaction allow dogs to communicate and live comfortably within the same household

Pugs are a popular choice for many families.

without repeated problems or conflicts in most cases. These normal dog behaviors can become problematic for owners who do not understand them. Families that are not prepared to train their Pug may be unable to tolerate or change normal dog behaviors such as barking.

Play Behaviors

Play behaviors are characterized by postures or vocal sounds that indicate a willingness to interact in a positive, playful manner. When young Pugs interact with human family members they often exhibit play behaviors as if they were playing with a littermate. Play behavior in dogs is one of social interaction and relationship building. The ability to play with other well-socialized dogs, accompanied by play with human family members, allows a puppy to learn problem-solving skills, provides necessary mental and physical stimulation, builds confidence, and teaches proper interaction skills.

Play Postures: The "play bow" is one of the most common body postures that a Pug uses to indicate a playful interaction. A Pug soliciting play will often drop onto his front legs, elbows on the floor, and subsequently lower his head, while keeping the rear end elevated, his tail uncurled and wagging during the display. This playful display may be accompanied by short, repetitive barking—the puppy's verbal attempt to say, "Play with me!"

Pugs are also noted for running through a room full speed ahead, with their back arched and their tail tucked, spinning and

The play bow is your Pug's way of saying "play with me!"

barking. They may jump on toys during the "fit" or lunge out to bite at anyone or anything within reach. They will stop to bark and then resume the "Pug run," seeming to gain momentum whenever their owners laugh at their antics. This behavior may seem unusual but it is a normal outlet for play energy in the Pug.

Play Biting: Play among puppies can include slamming into each other, chasing sequences, and biting—all of which are very normal play behaviors in dogs. They bite each other's ears, tails, feet, and legs during playful interactions. A very bold puppy may pin a less confident playmate by the back of the neck, growling and shaking the skin as if to say, "I'm the boss!"

Pug puppies are no exception when it comes to using their teeth during play. Play biting is one of the most common complaints from their owners. With or without socks, unsuspecting human toes become a target, taking the place of a littermate's ears and tail. Baggy clothing may also become a favorite plaything. Many Pug puppies also vocalize during play, growling whenever

their teeth find something to sink into. Barking, growling, and biting can all be part of normal play routines, but these common canine behaviors are often misinterpreted as aggressive or dominant actions by their owners. When a Pug puppy presents itself in a play bow, barking in a high-pitched tone and then begins to engage in biting toes or clothing, he is exhibiting normal play behaviors. This may escalate to growling once he has hold of a pant leg. Behaviors such as these normally decrease over time as the puppy matures. Chapter 8 offers ways to minimize your Pug's play biting.

Chewing

Dogs learn to explore their environments by observing their surroundings, using scent discrimination to investigate new objects, followed by an exploratory chew. If something warrants further investigation, a dog will often place the object in his mouth simply to find out what will happen. The chewing of objects satisfies a dog's natural curiosity, and is a primal instinct carried on from a dog's wild ancestors.

Chewing is a normal behavior for Pug puppies.

Chewing also serves as a means of relieving the discomfort caused by the eruption of puppy teeth. The desire to chew can also be an outlet for nervous or anxious behaviors, and is a normal way for a Pug to get rid of energy.

Canine Communication

Dogs have a complex language all their own. Their ability to send messages, receive and interpret signals, and respond to one another is nothing short of amazing. Teaching a Pug successfully requires knowing how to communicate your wishes in a language that he can understand.

Pugs, like all other dogs, do not inherently understand human words. In order to communicate in "dog language" you must first understand how dogs communicate with each other and reproduce those skills effectively during training.

Social Hierarchies

Dogs are a social species and are most at ease in a home that provides them with stable opportunities for socialization. These social relationships, or hierarchies, have a direct effect on a dog's behavior. Communication between members of the social family occurs constantly, using body language and vocal sounds to reinforce each member's position within the hierarchy.

Each individual within a dog's canine family or pack assumes a role or ranking position. Those individuals who are assertive and confident assume a domi-

nant role, or leadership position. Individuals who do not display confident behaviors or are nervous or fearful are looked upon as subordinates. Within any given social family, an individual may assume a dominant role over some members, but quickly assume a subordinate role with other more confident individuals.

When a Pug puppy enters a human family, people become his pack or littermates. A great deal of time is spent observing each individual's behavior, watching body language and listening to different voices, in an effort to determine his or her role in the hierarchy. Each time there is an interaction with this new family, the puppy is learning either to assert himself into a dominant role or act submissively, due partly in response to how the human individuals act and react. Adults often produce a submissive response from a puppy, while children may be viewed as subordinates. These "lower-ranking" individuals may quickly become a target for manipulative or play behaviors from the puppy, such as nipping and biting.

Body Language

The majority of canine communication is done through observation of body language, particularly facial expressions. Leaders in a canine hierarchy clearly exhibit confident body language, such as standing tall with erect ears and tail and making direct eye contact, while subordinates assume a posture that is lowered, avoiding eye contact and dropping their tails. A dog who wishes to display submission or avoid a confrontation may try to position himself under another dog's chin, and lick at the dog's lips or chin. He then rolls over on his back, presenting his belly to the more dominant individual. He may also lower his head and urinate submissively, a clear signal in dog language that he assumes a subordinate role to the approaching individual.

Human family members who are tall or have deep voices are at an advantage, as they are often automatically perceived by their Pugs to be in a leadership role. It is not uncommon to hear of Pugs who "only listen to the husband." These dogs believe men to be in a leadership role because their body posture and deep vocal patterns are recognized as strong leadership signals. These same individuals are often the unhappy recipients of a Pug puppy's submissive urination each time the puppy is approached.

Correctly interpreting the body language of some family members may be somewhat difficult for a puppy. Remember that your young Pug is constantly observing his new family trying to adapt to his new social hierarchy. Women often exhibit body language that quickly changes from a leadership position to subordinate and then back to leader. The nurturing or "mothering" instinct that many women have—constantly picking the puppy up to hug it or bending down to give it affection—may conflict with their attempts to reprimand or control the puppy. Children, especially infants and toddlers, exhibit body language that the puppy may believe is consistent with a littermate or subordinate. They often find themselves on the floor at the eye level of the puppy, and their uncoordinated movements may be perceived as submissive body language

Children may become a Pug's favorite play partner.

or a signal for play. Children who have high pitched voices often stimulate play behaviors in a Pug puppy.

Vocalization

Vocalization is a dog's way of communicating how he feels at any given moment or in a specific situation. A dog can express positive feelings such as greetings and pleasure using vocalization; he can also communicate fear, anxiety, and pain. Vocalization is the only way a dog can communicate at a distance from another of its own species.

The dog's normal vocal repertoire consists of barks, whines, and growls. Whining is quite often the first sound that a puppy learns to make, bringing mom back

Submissive Pugs often lick at the chin or lips of a more dominant dog.

to check out what is wrong. Pleasurable experiences may elicit a series of high-pitched, rapid barks or infantile whining and whimpering. Fear-based vocalization may include growling and barking, as does normal play behavior among litter-mates or playmates.

Verbal Communication

Most people communicate effectively primarily using their verbal skills. For dogs, verbal communication is usually a secondary form of communication. This difference between our species creates a communication nightmare for a Pug. Human language is completely foreign to a Pug. While dogs can learn to associate specific words for specific tasks, they do not automatically recognize the words themselves. Instead when a specific word

cue is used to mark a behavior, over time the Pug learns to associate that word with the behavior.

Dogs communicate with sounds that vary in pitch, tone, and frequency. Human verbal communication is rather monotone and boring to a dog. In order to help your Pug understand what you are trying to communicate, try to remember to use varying pitches and tones that correspond to the signal you want your Pug to process and understand. For example, in dog language, high-pitched tones indicate play behavior or something fun and exciting. Remember that normal canine play behaviors are accompanied by high-pitched barking patterns. With their high-pitched voices, children often inadvertently stimulate a Pug to play just by screaming or laughing. Praising your Pug for a job well done should be done in an upbeat tone of voice. You can mark a good behavior by verbally rewarding your Pug with an excited, *"Good job!"*

Words or sounds that are delivered in a sharp, descending tone of voice tend to inhibit motion in the Pug. The word *"no"* is often used ineffectively to try to stop a Pug from chewing on something inappropriate or to stop play biting. But the word itself means nothing to a Pug. When it is delivered in a sharp manner with a slight growl to it, the puppy recognizes the tone as a signal to stop, and may momentarily halt its behavior. Over time, if the word *"no"* is consistently spoken with the same deep, growling tone, the puppy will recognize it as a correction. By changing your voice to a low, growling tone you may be able to stop your Pug's bad behaviors, immediately receiving a more

Barking is a normal form of communication for Pugs.

Pugs were bred to be companions. They are most comfortable when they have a consistent role within a family and can count on endless hours of physical interaction with family members. A Pug's ability to fit in with his human family can be dependent on a variety of factors, including

■ social skills that a Pug has learned by interacting with littermates and adult dogs;
■ the ability of the human family to communicate using body language and vocal patterns that the Pug already understands;
■ the ability of the human family to recognize behaviors that are good;
■ properly timed rewards given to the Pug for good behaviors;
■ and proper managment of the Pug's environment to limit his ability to learn bad behaviors.

subordinate signal from the puppy. This will allow you to redirect him into a more positive behavior while strengthening your role as a leader.

You and Your Pug

Having a Pug as your companion can be a constant source of joy, bringing a smile to your face each time he greets you at the door. But when a Pug is improperly socialized, poorly trained, or living as an independent entity within a family, the relationship changes and living with him can be a challenge. Establishing the ability to effectively communicate with your Pug should be one goal every member of the family tries to achieve from the very moment the Pug joins the family.

Bonding

The relationship between a Pug and his owner is often referred to as the "bond" between them. Pugs develop a strong bond with their owners. In return, most Pug owners are sensitive to their Pug's every need. This bonding occurs during the first few weeks of the new relationship, especially when the Pug is an impressionable puppy.

While humans are capable of expressing a wide range of emotions, dogs are quite limited in how they can express their feelings. Bonding can mean different actions or behaviors to different people. To a Pug, however, the bond becomes strongest if all of the human family members display body

Pugs are a girl's best friend.

language and verbal signals that are easily read by the Pug, consistently delivered and appropriate for the context of the interaction. Inconsistencies in how an owner responds to a given situation, variations in training techniques by an individual, or harsh punishments can leave a Pug confused, anxious, and uncertain about his role within the family.

Leadership

Most Pugs are not born to be leaders. In fact, the majority would prefer to assume a subordinate role in life and are quite content with following their humans from the couch to the refrigerator, and then off to bed. Conflicts occur when owners fail to consistently behave in the role of a leader, or when a Pug is given regular opportunities to assert himself over family members or situations.

Leaders are confident and calm. Leaders do not raise their voices unnecessarily. Leaders have a clear idea of what their expectations of behavior are and they are able to communicate their wishes clearly and consistently, with sounds and actions that are delivered in a manner that a Pug can correctly understand.

Expectations From Your Trained Pug

When the comments are good, Pug owners love to have the dog everyone in the neighborhood talks about. No one wants to be the owner of the Pug the neighbors avoid because of bad behavior. Knowing how you want your Pug to behave is the first step to making your Pug the neighborhood darling.

Picture your Pug as you see him in the future. What behaviors do you want him to learn? What behaviors do you want him to avoid? You and your Pug will have a better relationship, and ultimately be much happier, if you teach him what you want him to do right from the beginning. Don't wait for him to display a bad behavior, getting irritated or angry when it occurs, and then expect him to behave in some other way. Being a leader means being proactive and committed to training your Pug!

Pug Myths

Many people erroneously believe that all toy breeds are difficult to live with, cannot be trained like larger dogs, or require

Pugs are always amusing!

special treatment. As one of the largest members of the toy group the Pug is often owned by individuals who never thought that they would consider owning a small dog. The Pug has a reputation for stealing the hearts of his owners, almost turning the tables on the relationship of who is in charge. The Pug has an uncanny ability to be amusing and it is his comical nature that often leads an owner to believe that Pugs are somehow different, unwilling, or unable to follow direction.

Myth One: Pugs Are Stubborn

By nature, Pugs are a very social breed. Each Pug has its own personality, one that is determined by a unique combination of genetic characteristics and the lessons learned from early socialization and experiences. Pugs as a whole are no more obstinate or stubborn than many other breeds. While it is true that some other breeds are more enthusiastic when it comes to learning, the Pug actually enjoys the interaction of participating in any activity with its owner. Historically the Pug's purpose as a lapdog predisposes him to be somewhat lazy when it comes to matters that do not involve food or affection.

The Pug may be mistakenly labeled as stubborn when in reality the owner simply is unable to communicate clearly in a manner that the Pug understands. The owner may be inconsistent in delivering commands or may not have a clear image of the behavior that is being taught. Pugs are intelligent and willing to learn, as long as

the message is clear and there is a reward for performing the desired behavior.

Occasionally an underlying medical condition can cause a Pug to be reluctant to perform certain tasks or seem unmanageable. Orthopedic problems can cause pain when performing simple tasks such as sitting or lying down. Eye injuries can be extremely painful, can cause visual deficits, and may permanently affect a Pug's ability to perform. Ear infections may limit a Pug's hearing and his lack of eagerness to listen to his owner may be due to deafness, not stubbornness.

Myth Two: Pugs Are Not Obedient

A dog's desire to be obedient is not only determined by his breed, but also his owner's leadership skills. A dog's compli-

Home Schooling

The *watch* command helps to teach Pugsley how to focus on you.

1. Begin with Pugsley standing directly in front of you in a quiet location.
2. Touch Pugsley's nose and give the command "Pugsley Watch." Move your hand slowly from Pugsley's nose toward your nose.
3. As Pugsley follows your hand and looks up at your face, verbally reward him with a "Good boy" and immediately give him a yummy treat as a bonus reward.
4. Practice this behavior each day, slowly increasing the length of time between the command and the verbal reward.
5. Now that Pugsley has learned how to focus, you should begin to practice this behavior in locations that have greater distractions. With any increase in distractions you will need to go back to immediately rewarding focus and then gradually increase the length of time before the reward.

ance can be directly influenced by two factors: focus and motivation. Dogs that are focused on their owners seem more eager to learn and appear to be more obedient.

A Pug that has learned to focus on his owner can be less challenging to work with, and therefore seemingly taught more easily. Pugs are not dumb. They are, however, very inquisitive, and that curiosity can lead to a temporary loss of focus.

If a Pug seems less than willing to obey his owner, the problem may not be outright disobedience. The defiance may be due to a lack of motivation. Motivating a Pug can be as easy as using a favorite food treat or providing a pleasant ear rub at the right time.

Myth Three: Pugs Cannot Perform

The success of Pugs in many different performance venues undeniably refutes the myth that Pugs cannot excel in performance events or competitions. Pugs have become a favorite partner of agility competitors and obedience exhibitors, often giving more enthusiastic breeds a run for the top spots. There has been at least one Pug with a tracking title, as well as several Pugs that currently participate in Canine Freestyle, a new and exciting event that combines traditional obedience commands with a dance routine.

The endless number of videos on the Internet featuring performing Pugs also provides evidence that Pugs not only are capable of performing, but often thrive in the spotlight. Pugs are clowns by nature and their antics often give their owners a reason to smile, laugh, and showcase their talent. They have enjoyed great success competing in canine talent shows, on television, and in film.

A Pug's ability to participate in any event is limited only by his owner's willingness to be involved. Any reluctance to participate or fear of failure will be recognized by your Pug. When you are intimidated or nervous, your Pug may also

Pugs have a reputation for being lazy.

become nervous or uneasy and fail to perform to his potential.

Myth Four: Pugs Can't Be Housebroken

Bring up the subject of housebreaking in a room full of Pug owners and you are sure to get a few uneasy chuckles. Many Pugs are notorious for leaving presents for their owners, while others will tell you that the Pug is one of the cleanest dogs that they have ever owned.

The Pug should be no more difficult to housetrain than any other toy breed. They can be housebroken easily as long as you are consistent in your training. Many apartment-dwelling Pugs have been successfully litter box trained. Housebreaking

failures are quite often an owner-created problem, not the result of a difficult Pug.

Chapter 6 deals specifically with housebreaking and confinement training. Using the strategies outlined in this chapter you should find that housebreaking your Pug is not difficult or impossible.

Myth Five: Pugs Can't Wear Collars

This myth results from misinformation, fear, and misguided intentions. Pugs can wear collars and many would be better behaved if their owners would put them on their Pugs and learn how to use them properly.

There is a mistaken belief that collars somehow predispose a Pug to breathing

Contrary to popular belief, Pugs can wear collars.

problems. While it is true that Pugs can be genetically predisposed to respiratory issues, a collar that is properly fitted does not increase the risk. Poor or non-existent training often results in a Pug that pulls continuously against the collar, causing the dog to choke, cough, or gag. These results are not caused by the collar, but are the result of a Pug who hasn't learned how to properly walk on a lead.

Collars offer more control than a harness and can be used to hold identifica-tion tags. The many patterns, colors, and textures available give you the opportu-nity to express your Pug's unique person-ality through his wardrobe.

Obesity and age can predispose a Pug to upper respiratory problems such as a col-lapsing trachea, diabetes, and congestive heart failure. For those Pugs that have been diagnosed with a respiratory prob-lem, a harness should be used. A harness should also be considered if a Pug has a his-tory of pulling or slipping out of a collar.

2 *The History of the Pug*

From the Beginning

The Pug is one of the world's oldest recorded breeds with a history that can be traced back as far as 551 B.C. The Pug is of Chinese origin and its early ancestor is believed to have been the Lo-Sze, or Chinese Foo Dog. The Lo-Sze was a dog of small size, and many of the characteristics of the Lo-Sze are still found in the Pug today.

The wrinkling in the forehead of the Pug was one of the hallmarks of the ancient Lo-Sze. The wrinkles of prized specimens formed a "W," or "Prince Mark," the Chinese character for "Prince." Although commonly docked, the tail of the Lo-Sze was also reported to have been curled before the procedure. The Lo-Sze's two distinct ear types are today known as the "button" and "rose" ears in the Pug and both breeds share a close-fitting, short coat.

Oriental Influences

The ancestors of the early Pug were worshipped by Chinese Emperors. The breed was considered one of their most prized possessions and many enjoyed the luxury of guarded rooms and servants who attended to their every need. As early as the 1800s, the Lo-Sze was being developed into the blueprint for the modern Pug. Breeding records describe short-coated Lo-Szes in a variety of colors. Black puppies were considered a symbol of bad luck and were often destroyed, while puppies of other colors were kept as treasured companions.

Royal Treatment

The love affair with the Pug did not end with the emperors in the Far East. The Pug's royal history dates back many centuries and is widely recorded throughout Europe. From Prince William of Orange in the late 1500s to the Duke and Duchess of Windsor in the early twentieth century, the Pug has been adored by many of Europe's royalty. Napoleon's wife, Josephine, adored her Pug, Fortune. Queen Victoria was also smitten by the "Pug Bug." Pugs have also been a part of the royal families in Russia and Holland.

The Pug's purpose as a lapdog and faithful companion has also made her a favorite of artists. William Hogarth's Pug, Trump, appeared in one of his paintings of 1730, and a Pug was included in one of

The Pug is one of the oldest breeds of dogs.

Spanish painter Francisco Goya's portraits of the late 1700s. French and German sculptors have immortalized the breed in their works, and the love affair with the Pug has continued into the modern era.

Popularity Concerns

The Pug has always enjoyed a favorite place in the hearts of its admirers. Celebrities of today continue to show off their Pugs, and Pug ownership is relished by everyone from actors and recording artists to race car drivers. Modern technology has made it even easier for the Pug to

enjoy a steady rise in popularity and for Pug owners to share their Pug's antics with other Pug lovers. The Internet today is full of home videos of Pugs doing everything from praying to singing. There are Pugs who "talk" and Pugs who can play dead. Each video demonstrates the Pug's gift of captivating her owner, as well as her aptitude for learning.

The Pug's popularity also has its disadvantages. Individuals who fall in love with the Pug's looks or antics as they are portrayed in the media often rush to own a Pug without really researching the breed or giving thought to whether they should be adding a dog to their life at all. The increased demand for Pug puppies has made them an easy target for unscrupulous breeders, who have little concern for producing healthy puppies or the care of those puppies after they are sold, and are simply interested in making money off of the popularity of the breed. The increasing number of Pugs who are seemingly difficult to train are a result of poor opportunities for socialization and poor training by owners who lack the time and commitment to work with their pets.

PUG POINTER
The Pug's likeable nature and unique personality have made it a favorite breed to include in television and movies. From the animated character, Percy, in Walt Disney's Pocahontas to the sarcastic Frank the Pug in Men in Black and Men in Black II, the Pug is fittingly portrayed as a companion dog that sometimes has a mind of its own.

3 *Selecting the Right Pug*

Good Dogs, Good Choices

The addition of a Pug to your family can be a wonderful event. The breed is known for longevity and it is not uncommon for a Pug to live to be 14 to 16 years of age. If your Pug is to become a well-behaved family member for years to come, selecting just the right Pug for your family is an important first step in promoting a healthy, happy relationship.

Make a Commitment

Purchasing a Pug should never be a spontaneous decision. That adorable "puppy in the window," purchased on a whim, will grow up quickly. On his journey to adulthood he will demand your undivided attention, interrupt your full night of sleep, and, at times, test your patience.

The addition of a Pug to your household can be compared to living with a new baby. Your daily routine will change dramatically. No more staying out late after work or long days of shopping. Your new Pug requires a firm schedule that provides for his need to sleep, play, and eliminate. You will need to plan for accommodations for your Pug when you schedule family vacations or long weekend getaways.

You must decide what his boundaries will be, and be patient while he learns about his new family and home. Your

family must work together to accomplish goals that everyone understands, and everyone must be willing to pitch in and be a part of the training process.

Your personal belongings will be subjected to puppy's teeth and paws. Housebreaking takes time and your expensive Oriental rug may become your Pug's favorite indoor potty spot if you can't commit the time to supervising him.

You must also be able to afford your Pug's medical care, food, toys, and other necessities. Pugs are plagued with their fair share of medical problems. The expense of treating health issues, such as recurrent eye and ear problems, can be great. Yearly physical exams, vaccinations, and medications all add up. You must ask yourself whether or not you can realistically afford to care for your Pug now—and in the future.

Is the Timing Right?

If you are considering a new Pug puppy, first ask yourself if you really have the time to devote to making him a well-behaved dog. A well-mannered adult Pug starts out as a silly, curious puppy. The metamorphosis to respectful companion

PUG POINTER
Pugs are great with children, but parents need to closely supervise any young child's play with a Pug. The Pug's exposed eyes are very vulnerable to injury from small fingers. Scratches to the eye can lead to serious problems including loss of the eye or blindness.

can only happen if you can afford to spend the time teaching your Pug puppy the behaviors that you want him to learn.

Adding a young to adolescent Pug to your life also requires a significant amount of dedicated time. A fully housebroken Pug only becomes a reality when the owner can adequately supervise him for many months. Troublesome or destructive adult behaviors are often perfected by young Pugs who have been left alone by owners who are too busy to notice. Pugs are very creative and often find ways to amuse themselves that do not always please their owners.

Adult Pugs who are searching for a new home may have special training needs. While you may bypass some of the behaviors that are associated with mischievous puppies, older puppies may have been poorly socialized, left alone frequently, or allowed to run the household, creating a greater need for structure and consistent training. Changing behaviors in adult Pugs can be difficult, and the amount of time needed to work with some of these Pugs may actually be greater in the long term than the initial time commitment of training a puppy.

Pugs for Kids

Many well-intentioned families wait to add a Pug until they believe that their children can help with the day-to-day responsibilities that come with owning a dog. While children may be excited about helping in the beginning, the care and training of a Pug should never be solely the responsibility of any child. The novelty of a new dog wears off quickly, and when

All children should learn how to properly interact with their Pug.

a child's interest moves on to other activities, it's the Pug who suffers.

A Pug's small size makes him ideal for life with children of all ages, but his basic needs often exceed the time, energy, and patience of even the most responsible child. That leaves the responsibility of training the Pug to mom and dad, who may struggle to fit the added burden into an already hectic schedule.

Pug puppies love to play with children. Unfortunately, normal puppy play often involves biting and nipping. You must be committed to supervising all play between your Pug puppy and your children, and teach your puppy how to interact with his human family. Perhaps more importantly,

you must also be committed to teaching your children how to interact appropriately with their new puppy, and that rough play that involves ear pulling, tail pulling, or grabbing fur and skin will not be tolerated.

Mature Pugs who didn't have the benefit of being loved by a child when younger may be intimidated by children. Younger children may inadvertently fall on or near your Pug, resulting in a Pug who is frightened and feels the need to be defensive. Adult Pugs who learned to assert themselves as adolescents may guard food or toys when children are playing nearby. Aggression is rare in Pugs, but any form of aggression is difficult to

PUG POINTER

Aggression is not a behavior that can be "trained" out of a dog. Aggressive dogs require intervention from a veterinary behaviorist or professional dog trainer, combined with the owners' management of the situations causing the aggressive response. Do not attempt to physically correct an aggressive Pug or teach him "who is boss." This can escalate the aggression, making the problem worse.

live with, can result in a child being bitten, and should not be tolerated.

Type and Temperament

For centuries, Pugs have been bred for a single purpose—to provide companionship to those who love them. The Latin phrase *multum in parvo* ("a lot in a little") is used in the breed standard to describe the adult Pug. Pugs bred with this standard in mind reflect the easygoing, laid-back temperament that has long been associated with the breed.

Pugs have continued to increase in popularity on a steady basis. But as has been the trend with many other popular breeds, this rise to stardom comes with a heavy price. With demand comes an increase in poorly bred Pugs with unsound temperaments. Popular breeds often suffer when unscrupulous or uninformed individuals begin to produce puppies in large numbers, using quantity, rather than quality, as a measurement of breeding

stock. "Teacup" Pugs, often bred from undersized or unhealthy parents, are now being advertised on many Web sites, though no such type of Pug exists according to the breed standard.

Over the past decade, many areas of the United States have seen a definite change in temperament related to the "type" or overall structure of Pugs. Owners who have purchased Pugs from breeders who strive to produce healthy Pugs with the smaller, square bodies, that conform to the breed standard, find that those puppies tend to grow up to be more laid-back, with a personality perfectly suited for a home companion. Thinner, leggier, "super-sized" Pugs are often more hyperactive and more independent. As adults, many of these Pugs lack the

Puppies should be purchased from experienced and reputable breeders.

Pugs come in only two recognized colors: fawn and black.

features that make the Pug unique, such as the flat, pushed in nose or dark, round eye. They are often referred to as "Victorian Pugs" or of "Victorian type." Their owners still love them, but many will admit that their Pug's behavior wasn't what they expected from the breed.

Color Differences

Pugs are generally recognized in two colors: fawn and black. Both colors make excellent pets; however, some Pug owners and breeders feel that subtle differences in personality and trainability can be related to color.

Fawn Pugs seem to have a more carefree attitude and are often described as clown-like. A fawn Pug may react to a sit-uation without really thinking, preferring to have fun and then to see what happens. Those owners and breeders dedicated to black Pugs often refer to them as "thinkers." Black Pugs appear to stop and analyze a situation and take a more studious approach to life. Perhaps this perceived personality difference between the colors is related to the larger population of fawn Pugs. While black coat color is the dominant gene, fawn Pugs have always been the more popular color.

One of the Pug's most appealing features are his facial expressions. At times, a Pug looks at you as if almost human, trying desperately to understand every word that you say. The color contrast of the ears, forehead, and muzzle that is present in fawn Pugs is lost in Pugs who are black. This lack of contrast takes away the black

Both male and female Pugs can make great pets.

Pug's ability to create the same facial expressions, which perhaps explains why some Pug owners and breeders believe that the black Pug is more serious.

Whether you prefer black or fawn, you will find that color has little or no influence on the trainability of your Pug. Both colors can excel in performance events, as therapy dogs, show dogs, or simply as couch potatoes!

Male vs. Female

People tend to have strong personal opinions as to whether a male or female Pug is better suited to be a family pet. Quite often, this bias is based on some past personal experience and reflects problems or concerns that occurred with another dog. We hear others tell tales about their dogs, their behavior problems, their successes and failures, and wrongly assume that a Pug of the same sex may be just as problematic. A specific sex within many breeds may have a predisposition to behavioral problems, but that does not mean that every breed has the same correlation.

A preference for female Pugs seems to be more common. This may reflect a misconception that all male dogs "mark" or leg lift inappropriately. While inappropriate marking behavior is often associated with male Pugs that are intact, neutered at a later age, or incompletely housebroken, female Pugs can also exhibit this behavior.

Choosing a female Pug does not eliminate potential housebreaking issues.

A Pug is a lapdog, bred to provide endless hours of companionship and love. Once again, many owners believe that this takes a "lady's touch." Don't underestimate the affection of the boys! Male Pugs often freely display more outward affection than their female counterparts, making them a favorite of many breeders and owners.

Determining which sex is right for you will be a matter of personal preference, unless your family already has a canine member. The sex of the Pug should be carefully considered when adding to a household that already has a dog. Pugs of both sexes can have very strong personalities, and these are often reflected in their interactions with other dogs. To avoid continual conflicts between housemates, it may be a good idea to add a Pug that is the opposite sex from your current dog. When it comes to conflict between two dogs in a household, female Pugs will often prove more troublesome than male Pugs.

Pugs are like potato chips—you can't have just one.

Double Trouble

There is a saying among Pug owners that "Pugs are like potato chips; you can't have just one!" Many Pug owners eventually have more than one Pug at a time, as the breed can become quite addicting. Working families often think about purchasing two puppies at the same time. They realize that the puppy will spend a significant amount of time alone during the day, and to minimize the loneliness, they believe that a second Pug puppy, perhaps two littermates, would do quite nicely. They also believe that the time it takes to train two puppies really would not be much more than the time needed to train one. Oh how wrong they are!

Properly raising two puppies is much more difficult than raising one. Puppies close in age, brought into the same household together, will always bond to each other before they bond to their human family. There is little or no incentive for them to bond with you or your children, as most, if not all, of their social needs are met by the other puppy. You simply become their source of food and a place to sleep. Housebreaking is also infi-

A well-socialized puppy becomes a well-behaved adult.

puppy's individual needs. Raising them correctly means that each puppy will still spend some time alone each day, defeating the original purpose for buying two puppies. You really need to ask yourself this question: *If adding a Pug puppy to my family means that he needs a canine sibling in order to be happy and healthy, should I really be contemplating the addition of a puppy at this time?*

Socialization

There are two important goals to shoot for when purchasing a Pug puppy. The first is to purchase a puppy that has the best chance to live a normal life, free from disease and hereditary conditions. The second is to select a puppy with a stable, social temperament. A properly socialized Pug puppy has the temperament to tackle any "job" he is given. Whether he is to spend his life as a beloved family pet, perform in obedience or agility competitions, or provide affection to others as a therapy dog, he must have the confidence to interact with people and be comfortable in locations outside of his own home.

nitely more difficult. Unless each puppy is treated independently, with adequate time separated from the other, their constant interactions and play behaviors increase the need for frequent potty breaks. Properly supervising two active Pug puppies is nearly impossible!

The only way to raise two puppies at the same time is to remember that they are individuals—not one puppy with eight legs. This means two of everything! Two crates, two leashes and collars, two sets of food and water dishes, and double the time and expense! You must be able to budget the time and energy to meet each

How a puppy is treated *before* he joins your family directly influences your puppy's ability to learn. Critical periods of development occur at specific ages in a puppy's life. If a puppy is too stressed during these sensitive periods, it can negatively influence his trainability for even the simplest tasks can be negatively influenced.

Pug puppies separated from littermates before eight weeks of age miss the opportunity to learn about interactions with

PUG POINTER

Obedience classes with a curriculum geared specifically toward puppies aged ten weeks to six months are offered by kennel clubs, boarding and training kennels, veterinary clinics, and local park districts. These classes, known as Puppy Kindergartens or Puppy Socialization, teach basic obedience commands while offering your Pug puppy a chance to play with other dogs of similar age.

Puppy classes are a terrific way to socialize your Pug properly after you bring it home. A well-run class provides a safe environment for your puppy to play in, and gives you an early way to begin training your Pug.

A properly run puppy class has a maximum of six to eight puppies per instructor and is located in a space that is large enough to accommodate safe play. The instructors should be knowledgeable about dog behavior, proper dog training techniques, and be able to communicate these in a clear manner. The curriculum should include instruction on how to handle common puppy problems, basic obedience commands, and should be taught in a positive manner.

other dogs. Social interactions with humans should begin as early as three to five weeks of age. By nine weeks of age, puppies form a distinct preference for the location of elimination (inside vs. outside) and for the surface they prefer to eliminate on (newspaper, grass, concrete, gravel). The exploration period, when puppies are comfortable learning about new places and objects, begins as early as ten weeks of age, and continues until a puppy reaches four to five months of age.

Using these guidelines, you can begin to understand why some Pugs may be difficult to housebreak, anxious about new people or places, and appear to learn more slowly than others. Some Pug puppies may be slow to housebreak if they are only used to eliminating indoors, on newspapers, at twelve weeks of age. A Pug puppy with little contact with strangers before being sent to join his new home may always be apprehensive of new people. The Pug puppies offered through pet stores are usually separated from their littermates before eight weeks of age, which may make it difficult for them to properly interact with other dogs.

Positive new experiences need to continue after you bring your puppy home. Exposing your Pug to new people and places, and avoiding situations which may be too frightening or stressful, lays the foundation for your Pug puppy to accept new rules and succeed in becoming a well-trained Pug.

Where to Buy Your Pug

While Pugs have become more popular, their availability from reputable sources has not increased to meet the demand. Remember that what happens to your Pug before he joins your family can directly influence his training once he comes home. Choosing a Pug from the right source must be considered a part of the training process.

The Show Breeder

Purchasing a puppy from a show breeder can be a lengthy process. These breeders often keep puppies longer, as they observe them and continually evaluate their potential in the show ring. A show breeder is keenly aware of the Pug's health concerns, screening for genetic defects prior to breeding. They usually know the pedigree of their Pugs for many generations, and can share information about your puppy's grandparents and great-grandparents.

Show breeders do not produce a large number of litters in a year. It is not uncom-

Breeders of show Pugs can be a great source of information for a puppy buyer.

mon for a show breeder to have a waiting list for puppies, and many will require a deposit in order to reserve a puppy from a future litter. Show breeders seldom advertise in newspapers or on the Web. Most of their puppies are sold by referral from other puppy purchasers or other breeders.

Show breeders may also have older puppies or young adults that have been trained for the show ring, but for one reason or another, are not as competitive as the breeder had hoped. These Pugs are usually quickly acclimated to a new family and home, as their preparation for the show ring has previously exposed them to frequent handlings, new people, and storage environments. Show breeders' experience with Pugs, combined with their ability to properly care for and socialize puppies before they are sold, makes them the perfect option for purchasing your new Pug puppy.

To find a show breeder you should plan to attend a local dog show. The American Kennel Club (www.akc.org) can provide you with a list of upcoming shows in your area. Show breeders may appear to be difficult to talk to at first, especially if you approach them while they are waiting to enter the ring. Be patient and persistent. You should ask if there is a good time to ask them some questions. If you intend to compete with your Pug in any performance event, the show breeder can evaluate his or her puppies and provide you with the best candidate for your chosen activity. If you cannot attend a local dog show try contacting a kennel club in your area and ask for a breeder referral list. Local veterinarians may also be able to provide referrals.

Pug puppies can be hard to resist.

The Hobby Breeder

A hobby breeder is someone who breeds Pugs strictly for placement as pets. These breeders usually have one or two males and breed them to the female Pugs they own. Hobby breeders may produce several litters per year. They may also have limited knowledge about the health problems of the Pug, and may know very little about the Pugs in their puppies' pedigrees.

Puppies from hobby breeders are generally raised in the breeder's home. A hobby breeder may advertise in local papers, veterinary clinics, and on Web sites dedicated to puppy sales.

The Pugs used for breeding by hobby breeders are most often of the Victorian type, so it is important to observe both the mother and father. Victorian-type Pugs often lack the sedate, easygoing Pug temperament, one of the qualities that draw families to this breed. Their hyperactivity can make them a challenge to breed. The future behavior of your puppy will be influenced not only by the genetics inherited from mom and dad, but his observations of their behavior.

Pet Stores

Pet stores generally have Pugs available within a short period of time. If you are impatient and must have a puppy right away, a pet store may be your only option.

All pet stores purchase their puppies from commercial breeding operations. The puppies are usually sold through a middleman, known as a broker or wholesaler. These puppies are almost always separated from their littermates at an early age and may have been housed in poor conditions prior to arriving at the pet store. These factors can negatively affect a puppy's adaptability and train-ability in its new home.

The parents of pet store puppies sel-dom receive any screening for genetic health issues, and are used for breeding regardless of medical problems, type, or temperament. While it may be hard to resist a Pug puppy that looks at you with those big, sad eyes, it is important to remember that you have no knowledge of his background or breeding.

Newspaper Ads

Your local paper may contain advertise-ments for Pug puppies. These ads may be placed by hobby breeders, or puppy bro-kers, the very same people who supply the pet stores. You can distinguish where the puppies are from with a little observa-tion and by asking a few simple questions:

■ Check the phone number. If the same phone number appears several times, listed with several breeds of dogs, the puppies are being sold through a broker.
■ Ask the person who answers the phone if one or both parents are on the premises. A hobby breeder usually has them and will let you meet them. A broker only has puppies available for purchase. A broker may also indicate that the litter was bred in another state by a "friend" or "relative" and that they are trying to help sell the puppies.
■ Ask when you can come and see the puppies. A hobby breeder will set up a time for you to visit. A broker may offer to meet you halfway, usually in a park-ing lot, in a location they seem to know very well.

Puppies sold through brokers generally originated in facilities such as barns or outdoor pens that have poor conditions. Once again you will have no knowledge of the puppy's parents, and should a problem arise with your puppy in the future, you will often be unable to locate either the breeder or the broker who sold you the puppy.

Internet Sales

A fancy Web site does not necessarily indi-cate that the puppy is nicely bred, but the Internet can be a useful tool for locating a Pug breeder, if you know where to look.

Breeder referrals are offered by many kennel club Web sites; you can find them through the American Kennel Club (www.akc.org). The Pug Dog Club of America also provides a breeder referral contact (www.pugs.org).

If you choose to type in the words "Pug puppy" on a search engine, you'll be directed to hundreds of classified ads. You must do your homework, and know what to look for before agreeing to purchase a Pug via the Internet. Many of the com-mercial breeders supplying pet store chains also advertise via pretty Web sites. Another group of breeders, often referred to as puppy mills, have found the Internet to be a virtual gold mine for selling Pug puppies. These breeders produce many puppies each year, in conditions that are unsanitary, and providing only minimal care to the dogs used for breeding. So how do you know if the "breeder" listed on the Internet can provide your family with a suitable, healthy puppy? Ask these questions:

Like mother, like daughter—heredity can affect your Pug's trainability and health.

- Can I come and pick up my puppy? If a breeder will not allow you to see where the puppy has been raised, a red flag should go up.
- Can I have references from previous puppy buyers? Reputable breeders are happy to provide you with names and phone numbers of previous clients.
- May I have a copy of your guarantee and purchase contract to review? If a breeder will not provide these, or does not use them, do not purchase a puppy.

Humane Shelters and Rescue Organizations

If an adult Pug seems to be a better fit for your family, start your search by contacting your local humane society. Unfortunately Pugs do wind up in shelters; most are young adults desperately in need of a stable home that can provide training.

Pug rescue groups are located throughout the United States. These groups generally charge a nominal adoption fee and can be a great place to find an adult Pug to fit your family and lifestyle.

Local veterinary clinics can usually provide a list of shelters and rescue organizations in your area. You can also find many rescue groups online, or through The Pug Dog Club of America.

What to Look For

No matter where your search for a Pug leads you, it is up to you to be educated about your purchase. If you are looking for a puppy, you should ideally be able to visit the litter before the day arrives for you to take him home. Observe how each puppy acts and reacts to his littermates, human caregiver, and your family. A bossy,

Make sure that your Pug puppy appears healthy and happy.

out-of-control puppy may require a more assertive training program, and a more confident family. A shy puppy, one who always seems to move away from contact, will require a training routine that includes positive interactions and minimal stress after you take him home.

If you plan to have fun in obedience or agility, you will want a puppy that is active and observant, with an air of confidence about him. Self-confident Pug puppies make wonderful performance dogs.

Check each puppy carefully for any signs of illness or health problems. His eyes should be bright and clear, with no discharge, cloudiness, or protrusion evident. Check his ears by gently lifting the ear flap and taking a peek at the ear canal. It should be free from debris and dry, with no offensive odor. His nose wrinkle should also be clean and dry; if it is dirty, damp, or has a strong odor now, this condition will most likely be chronic. Every Pug puppy should be inspected by a licensed

veterinarian prior to being sold to a new owner, and should have received at least one vaccination. Ask for a health record with the veterinarian's name and the clinic name, address, and phone number.

Observe the overall body shape, condition, and structure of the puppies in the litter. Fat, roly-poly Pug puppies, with good body condition, become relaxed, properly proportioned adults. The legs should resemble tree trunks sturdy enough to support a square body. Legs on Pug puppies that look more like saplings are often seen on the Victorian-type Pugs. Those Pugs who have a future athletic career, running and jumping in agility, must be able to handle stress on their bones and joints, so structure and condition is of the utmost importance.

The location where the puppies are raised should be clean, well ventilated, and free from odor. Pug puppies that are raised in dirty, cramped cages or pens are often impossible to completely housetrain.

To Pick or Not to Pick

It is natural to fall in love with every Pug puppy you see, but there may be one puppy that really catches your eye, and tugs at your family's heartstrings. Is that puppy truly the right puppy for you? Show breeders will most likely select a puppy for you, based not only on your preferences, but more importantly, on their observations and evaluations of the litter, and your family's specific needs. An observant, responsible breeder can often pick the Pug puppy that best reflects the qualities your family truly needs. Pug puppies that are purchased from other sources are often sold on a first-come, first-sold basis. You may be forced to choose a puppy who, while cute and adorable, may not really be suited for your family, or leave empty handed.

An educated Pug buyer asks questions, requires the right answers, observes potential puppies, and, above all, uses common sense when making a final decision. While there is always the temptation to "rescue" a puppy if he looks ill, has been raised in unsanitary conditions, or is currently on medication with the "guarantee" he'll get better soon, it is in your family's best interest to decline the purchase. A healthy, robust Pug puppy gives you the best foundation for a healthy adult Pug.

Registration Papers, Contracts, and Guarantees

Registration papers, sales contracts, and guarantees can be very confusing to the new Pug owner. There are several independent registries that offer "papers," but are they all equal? Contracts and guarantees are as varied as the breeders and sellers who put them together.

What Are Papers?

Registration papers are simply a certificate that identifies your individual puppy by its sire (father) and dam (mother), birth date, and litter or individual registration number. Registration papers are *not* a guarantee of health or quality and they are *not* the same as a pedigree. A pedigree is your Pug's family tree, listing three to five generations of his ancestry.

The American Kennel Club, or AKC, has long been considered the gold standard of registries. The AKC offers registration of puppies, pedigree services, and inspection of breeders. The American Kennel Club is currently the only registry that offers a DNA program. The DNA program can be used to verify parentage, and Pugs that have been DNA tested will appear in a pedigree with their DNA number. The AKC also licenses kennel clubs, which promote conformation events and performance events. If you intend to show your Pug in conformation, agility, or obedience, your Pug puppy should have a litter registration from the AKC.

There are several other registries that offer papers for purebred Pugs. Show breeders will always offer AKC-registered Pug puppies for sale, but you may find puppies from other sources are registered with one of the following:

- Continental Kennel Club (CKC) offers registration of purebred Pugs, pedigree services, and limited performance event competitions.
- United Kennel Club (UKC) offers registration of purebred Pugs, pedigree services, and conformation and performance event competitions.
- American Dog Breeder Association (ADBA) offers registration of purebred Pugs only with a verifiable three-generation pedigree.
- American Pet Registry, Inc. (APRI), offers registration of purebred Pugs.
- Dog Registry of America offers registration of purebred Pugs and Pug mixes.

Because some of the registries will issue "papers" for Pugs without verifying a pedigree, it is possible that puppies that are registered and come with "papers" may not be purebred Pugs. If the puppy you purchase is not purebred he may not have the laid-back, amiable Pug personality.

Contracts

A purchase contract is a written agreement between the breeder or seller of a Pug puppy and the buyer. It should be

You may be able to pick your Pug puppy from a litter, or he might pick you!

Ask your breeder for a copy of your Pug's pedigree.

a requirement before you agree to purchase any Pug. Without a purchase contract, you will have no legal recourse should your new Pug become ill, or worse yet, die, from an inherited medical condition. A proper contract should include all of the following:

■ The breeder's name, address, and phone number.

■ The seller's name, address, and phone number (if seller is not the breeder).
■ The puppy's name, sex, date of birth, and color.
■ The puppy's breed and litter or individual registration number.
■ The sire's name and registration number.
■ The dam's name and registration number.
■ A short-term health guarantee.
■ A long-term health guarantee.
■ Replacement or refund information.
■ Buyer's name, address, and phone number.
■ Purchase price.
■ Requirements or obligations of the buyer.
■ Spay/neuter requirements.

If a written contract is not offered, it is buyer beware. You may be purchasing a puppy that is not purebred, or has a known medical condition. Reputable breeders always use a purchase contract and will provide a copy when asked. A written contract is a safeguard for both the buyer and the seller.

How Good Is a Guarantee?

Health guarantees should be a part of the written contract. A well-written contract, from a reputable breeder, will include both a short-term health guarantee, usually seven to ten days from the purchase date, and a long-term guarantee, usually one to two years from the puppy's date of birth.

The contract should clearly state what the breeder's responsibility is should your

Make sure that you are familiar with your Pug's health guarantee.

puppy become ill. Does she intend to replace the puppy, offer a full or partial refund, or pay for medical expenses? Which medical expenses are covered, and which are not, should be clearly stated. Will a second opinion, from a veterinarian of the breeder's choice, be required before any treatment is started?

As part of the guarantee, the contract should also list any specific requirements that you must fulfill as the puppy's new owner. Some breeders require an initial visit to a veterinarian within a specific period of time after you take your puppy

home. You may also be asked to feed a specific diet to your puppy, or give nutritional supplements. You may need to maintain receipts for those products, in order for the health guarantee to be valid.

If you should ever find it necessary to find a new home for your Pug, whether it is due to a personal issue or a behavioral problem, what is the breeder's responsibility? A contract should state whether or not the breeder will willingly take back your Pug should you be unable to take proper care of him or find that you can no longer live with him.

4 *Understanding Dog Training*

Obedience training can be a wonderful way to strengthen the bond that you have with your Pug. Working with your Pug does not have to be time-consuming or difficult; however, it does help to have a basic understanding of dog behavior before you begin. If you understand how your Pug learns, teaching him how to behave becomes as easy as learning your ABCs.

How Dogs Learn

The study of animal behavior gives us insight into how all creatures learn. Dogs are highly intelligent, social animals that learn to repeat behaviors that are rewarded. Your Pug is no exception. Your Pug is continuously learning, mastering both good and bad behaviors through repetition of his habits and patterns of behavior.

Behavioral science and its relevance to dogs is a field of study that has rapidly grown in the last two decades. There are differing theories as to how an animal learns. How these theories apply to dog training is a topic that continues to spark debate among animal behaviorists, veterinarians, dog trainers, and owners. Dog training techniques of the past often

relied on physical force or conflict to overpower and force dogs to behave. Research into animal behavior has changed the way many trainers work with dogs. Modern dog trainers use a much more positive, gentle approach to successfully change dog behavior.

Operant Conditioning

For most dog trainers, operant conditioning is the foundation for teaching dogs good behaviors. Based on the principle that the dog can control her environment by choosing to perform behaviors that are rewarded and to avoid behaviors that are punished, operant conditioning involves pairing something that is either good or bad with a specific behavior to either reinforce it or decrease its frequency. In other words, a dog learns to associate her own actions with a good or bad consequence. There are four principles of operant conditioning:

1. Positive reinforcement pairs the dog's behavior with something pleasant. The dog's behavior makes something good or desirable happen.
   Example: Dog sits and then receives a cookie.

33

Pugs can learn to behave if they have consistent direction from their owner.

change or create behaviors. Dogs had to make mistakes repeatedly in order to learn that they produced bad consequences, and then try to determine what made those consequences go away. Today's modern dog trainer focuses primarily on reward-based training, using positive reinforcement techniques to teach desirable behaviors.

Behaviors and Consequences

From your Pug's perspective, her actions result in a behavior, and every behavior has a consequence. The consequence of any behavior is viewed as either good or bad. Knowing that dogs will likely repeat behaviors that are rewarded, a good consequence increases the chances that your Pug will repeat the behavior again. A bad consequence means that the behavior is less likely to be tried again. Behaviors that are repeated often over time become learned behaviors.

Here is an example: Your Pug investigates the garbage can. She jumps on the garbage can, which falls over spilling out leftover food on the floor. The leftover food is eagerly eaten. The *action* of investigating the garbage can resulted in the *behavior* of jumping on the garbage can. The leftover food is a yummy treat or *good consequence* from your Pug's perspective. That means that she is likely to continue to investigate the garbage can on a regular basis.

Good consequences are known as rewards. Rewards can be anything that your Pug views as enjoyable. Remember

2. Positive punishment pairs the dog's behavior with something unpleasant. The dog's behavior makes something bad or undesirable happen.
   Example: Dog jumps up and receives a collar correction.
3. Negative reinforcement. The dog's behavior makes something unpleasant disappear.
   Example: Dog pulls on collar and begins to gag or choke. When dog sits, collar pressure is released.
4. Negative punishment. The dog's behavior makes something desirable disappear.
   Example: Dog barks while looking outside a window, resulting in the curtains being closed.

The old obedience training methods primarily involved the use of negative reinforcement and positive punishment to

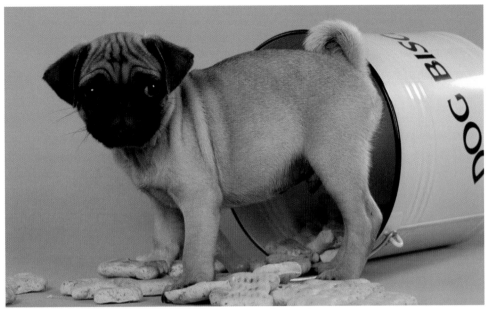

A Pug must be corrected while he is misbehaving, not afterwards.

that you are thinking from your Pug's point of view! Food is probably the most highly motivating reward for most Pugs, but there are many others. A favorite toy can be a reward; so can gaining your attention or getting a good belly rub. Your voice can be used to give a verbal reward. The words "good girl," spoken in an excited tone of voice, can become a highly valuable motivator. Many Pugs find that going for a walk or riding in the car is rewarding. And let's not forget sleeping in that cozy spot on the couch, a great perk for the "couch potato" Pug.

Bad consequences can vary depending on the situation or behavior. Any action, sound, or event that stops your Pug from continuing a behavior constitutes a cor-

REMOTE CORRECTION DEVICES

Remote correction devices can be used to change behaviors that occur away from you or out of your immediate control. They should be strong enough to stop the undesirable behavior, but not so aversive that they cause anxiety or injury. Some examples of remote correction devices are:

- *Squirt guns*
- *Air horns*
- *Soda can filled with coins (also called a shaker can)*
- *Anti-bark collars*
- *Remote training collars*
- *Underground fence systems*

Rewarding good behavior is the best way to train a Pug.

rection. Corrections can only be effective if they are given as, or immediately after (within a few seconds), a behavior occurs. Let's look at some consequences that your Pug might consider to be bad. A sharp, verbal sound, or the word "no" from you, might be enough to stop some behaviors but not others. A tug on the leash or a tightening on her collar are both examples of physical corrections.

What if your Pug's behavior neither produces a good consequence nor results in a particularly bad one? She may try the behavior again in an attempt to produce different results. Or she may try something different to get what she wants. Absence of any clear-cut benefit usually results in a slight modification in behavior by your Pug.

Bad behaviors are often repeated because your Pug has learned how to reward herself. For example, jumping on you or your guests quickly becomes a learned behavior because it always pro-

duces physical contact (a reward), may result in verbal communication that the Pug does not consider bad (another reward), and rarely produces any bad consequences.

Reward-based Training: Research has shown that the quickest way to change a dog's behavior is to use reward-based training techniques. This means that you will reward your Pug immediately when her behavior is positive or when she does something you want her to do. The reward makes it more likely that she will repeat that behavior in the future.

Good Timing

Knowing when to give your Pug positive reinforcement is the single most important factor in getting her to associate the reward with the desired action. When you are teaching your Pug to perform a desired behavior, the reward should be given *immediately* when the behavior occurs as well as every time the behavior is displayed. For example, your Pug will learn the *sit* command much more quickly if a reward is given every time her rear end hits the ground.

The same is true for corrections. Corrections should be consistent and occur immediately as the behavior is occurring. Corrections that occur after the fact may not be associated with the undesirable behavior, and therefore may be ineffective in changing your Pug's behavior.

Let's look at the garbage can scenario presented earlier in this chapter. If the behavior of jumping up on the garbage

can resulted in a loud crash and a lid prevented the contents from spilling out
onto the floor, the consequence would
not be a positive one. If the loud crash
was frightening to the Pug it could be
considered a correction. The result is that
the Pug would be less likely to investigate
the garbage can on a regular basis.

Reinforcing Good Behaviors

It is important that your Pug learn how
to associate her behavior with a pleasant
outcome. We know that to a Pug food is
a big reward, something that is likely to
reinforce her behavior. But we don't want
to have to carry dog treats with us all the
time in order to reward your Pug for her
good behavior. Wouldn't it be nice to be
able to reward her verbally and have it
mean something? Your Pug doesn't
understand that "good girl" means anything at first. If you deliver those words in
an upbeat tone of voice she will believe
that you are pleased based solely on the
vocal tone, not the words themselves.
Your Pug must first learn to associate
those two words with something rewarding in order to be able to understand it as
an effective reward in the future. This is
known as a conditioned reinforcer.

Children learn to associate a gold star
on a paper with a job well done. At first
the gold star means nothing. The teacher
may initially give the child a piece of
candy along with the paper with a gold
star. The candy is the reward at first. Eventually, over time, the child learns to associ-

Good behavior will start early if you reward and
praise your Pug.

ate the gold star as something positive
because it has been accompanied in the
past by a piece of candy. A conditioned
reinforcer is taking something that is neutral and making it as important or
rewarding as something that is already
considered high in value.

Clicker training in dogs, using a device
that makes a clicking noise to signal that
your Pug's behavior is correct, is one example of using a conditioned reinforcer to
reward specific behaviors immediately as
they occur. At first you'll use a food reward
in conjunction with the clicker. Begin by
giving your Pug the treat. Next, click the
clicker before giving the treat. Repeat this
several times each day. Your Pug will begin

to learn that the clicking sound indicates that a treat is coming, which is a positive outcome. Once she knows that the clicking sound precedes a treat, you can use it to reward good behavior. Clicker training has its drawbacks as you will have to have the clicker with you whenever you want to reward your Pug for good behavior. If you wish to compete with her in performance or companion animal events you will be unable to use a clicker in the ring and will have to change the way you reward her before you can compete.

Another conditioned reinforcer would be to use a phrase, such as *"good girl,"* instead of the clicker. To begin introducing your Pug to the concept of conditioned reinforcement, begin by pairing the words *"good girl"* with a food reward. Tell your Pug *"good girl"* and immediately give her the reward. Do this several times each day and pretty soon she will associate those two words with the treat. Once that connection is made you can begin to use those two words (your conditioned reinforcer) to help teach her when her behavior is correct.

Let's say you want to teach your Pug to greet you with all four feet on the ground. You have already taught him that "good girl" means a food reward is coming. Her initial greeting behavior is likely to be excitement and exuberance, greeting you by jumping up on your legs. You want to be prepared to reward your Pug when she has all four feet on the floor so pay attention to her movements. Stand quietly while she is jumping at you, or pawing at your legs. The instant all four feet are on the floor use your conditioned reinforcer (*"good girl"*) to mark the specific behavior

first, followed by the food reward. When delivered immediately as she is standing still, the reinforcer tells your Pug that standing, not jumping, is the desired behavior. The words also predict the food reward to follow. Repeat this exercise several times, making sure that you reward your Pug for having "four on the floor."

Intermittent or Variable Reinforcement

Once your Pug understands a behavior, it's time to begin to reward her on a random basis. Behaviors that are rewarded intermittently, both good and bad, are often the strongest behaviors a dog knows and, in the case of bad behaviors, can be the most difficult to change. When learned behaviors are rewarded on a random basis it makes your Pug try harder in order to receive the reward. The concept is the same as that behind a slot machine, the human's equivalent of intermittent reinforcement. We start by playing for a short time. If we do not win at all we become bored and move to something different. If we win a little back, we continue to put more money into the machine, hoping to be rewarded again. Winning even a little causes you to keep playing, hoping for more.

Let's use the "four on the floor" greeting again as an example. Each day when you are teaching your Pug what you want her to do instead of jumping, you will reward her immediately for the correct behavior with *"good girl"* and a food reward. As your training progresses you see that your Pug no longer jumps on you (she understands what is expected), quickly standing still in front of you instead (your reward-based training has taught her the behavior you desire). You can now begin to use only your conditioned reinforcer, *"good girl,"* to mark the behavior, and provide a food reward only fifty percent of the time. Your Pug should still greet you by having four on the floor. If she does not (jumps up at you, for example), try to ignore the behavior or turn away from her and be prepared to reward her as soon as she has her feet on the ground. This teaches your Pug to continue to try for the right behavior. After a short time you can reduce the food reward further, adopting a variable schedule of reinforcement. You can continue to use the verbal reward *every* time, because the conditioned reinforcer becomes the reason she is working for you!

Clues to Cues

Up until now we have focused on learning theories. Now it's time to put those theories into motion. How is your Pug supposed to know what the *sit* command means? Or for that matter, how does she know that when you say her name, you are talking to him? Remember that dogs communicate using body language and verbal cues. Your Pug needs to learn that there are signals that indicate a specific behavior. These signals are known as cues. Cues can be either visual or verbal. Hand signals and changes in body posture can become visual cues. Verbal commands are verbal cues for specific behaviors.

> **PUG POINTER**
>
> *Intermittent reinforcement can be effectively given on either a variable or a fixed schedule. As the names imply, variable schedules reward behaviors after a variable number of repetitions or after a variable length of time, while fixed schedules reward after a specific number of repetitions or a specific amount of time. Variable schedules of reinforcement statistically produce the highest level of correct responses.*

When you first brought your Pug home she didn't immediately know her name. Over time she learned that the verbal cue of calling her name meant that you were talking to her. Your body language and voice rewarded her for responding.

Lure Training

Many trainers begin teaching obedience commands by using food, wiggled or moved in a specific motion, to help the dog into the desired position. Once the desired behavior has occurred, the food is given as a reward. This method of training is known as luring or food-lure training. Food-lure training is one form of positive reinforcement training.

Target Training

One common problem with food-lure training is that the dog may learn to focus on the food first and only perform a task because she sees or smells the food. This problem can be solved by gradually

39

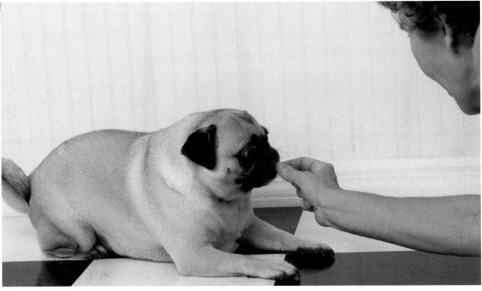

A small food reward between your fingers or in your closed fist can become a target.

removing food rewards while training, a process known as fading. Another alternative is to teach the dog by using a target instead of using food held between your fingers and thumb.

Teaching your Pug to identify a specific location or object, and then to focus intently on that location or object, is known as target training. The easiest way to begin this is to use your fist as the target. When taught properly, your Pug learns to recognize the target quickly and follow it into a behavior that eventually results in a food reward. When you first introduce the target, your Pug will receive a food reward every time she touches it. Once touching the target is mastered you can begin to give her food rewards on a random basis, or combine the target with

some other behavior that produces the food reward.

Begin by placing a small food reward in your hand and closing your hand around it to produce a fist. Rotate your hand toward the dog so that your fingers are facing him. Get her attention and encourage her to move toward the target. As soon as your Pug investigates your fist, touching it with her nose, verbally reward her using your conditioned reinforcer ("Good Girl"), and immediately open your fist to produce the food reward. Repeat this exercise several times in a row each day for at least a week. You can move your fist around to make your Pug work a little harder to touch the target as she starts to understand this exercise. Once she understands that the target produces something good you can use it to lure her into performing other behaviors, without having to show her the food reward first.

Physical Cues

Physical cues that mark specific behaviors are also called hand signals. A hand signal often results from luring the dog into performing a specific task. You can use hand signals to cue your Pug into a specific behavior. Hand signals are not universal and can vary from trainer to trainer. In order for your Pug to learn to associate your hand signals with specific behaviors, you must be consistent in their use.

Verbal Cues

When to add verbal cues to indicate a specific behavior is a subject of controversy. Traditionally, dog trainers gave a verbal command or cue as they lured or maneuvered the dog into the desired position. Some trainers advocate repeating the verbal cue or command many times while teaching an exercise, while other trainers feel that this causes a dog to tune out the verbal cues from the owner. Either way, if your Pug is rewarded immediately when the desired behavior occurs, she should learn to associate the verbal cue with the action.

Other trainers prefer to teach a behavior first and then add the verbal cue once the desired behavior is being performed. The reason for this is based on animal behavior theories that the dog learns to associate verbal cues with a specific behavior much more quickly when the desired behavior is already mastered. Since indi-

Training is easy when you are in a good frame of mind.

vidual Pugs learn at different speeds, you can try each technique to see if one way produces a faster response. There is no right or wrong way to introduce verbal cues. Your Pug should be able to learn verbal cues as long as the reward is given immediately for the desired behavior.

Body Language Cues

Because body language is such an important form of communication among dogs, your Pug may learn to read yours without even having a lesson. Dogs are very adept at looking at human body posture and facial features and making a judgment call on what they mean. Your body posture is a cue to whether you are happy, sad, worried, angry, or afraid. You can use your body language to let your Pug know when she has done something good by smiling at her, opening your arms wide, or by giving her a pat on the head or a scratch behind the ears. As you scold her for destructive behavior your muscles tighten and your face hardens. This change in your body posture is a distinct clue that you are unhappy.

When you are training your Pug it is important to make sure that your body language reflects your attitude. If you are in a bad mood you are less likely to smile and your muscles may be much more tense. This body language may make your Pug uncomfortable or afraid to try new behaviors, or more hesitant to perform. Teaching new behaviors may be difficult

You can recognize an unhappy Pug by her uncurled tail.

if your Pug is concerned that you are displeased with her.

Your body language must also be consistent with the message you are trying to deliver. Teaching the *stay* on command may take longer if you consistently bend over your Pug and she reads this signal as an invitation to *come* instead. Crossing your arms in front of you makes your body appear stiff and is a great body language cue for the *stay* exercise. If your Pug is jumping on you consistently, check to see if you are bending over her when she greets you. You may have inadvertently trained her to do this as a puppy by bending over when you picked her up (physical reinforcement following a distinct body language cue).

Pug Body Language

When training, you should also learn to read your Pug's body language. Pugs use body language effectively to communicate just how they are feeling. Pugs have a reputation for being slow learners, perhaps because few people learn to read their body language. Pugs have some unique ways to let you know whether or not they are enjoying a training session.

A Pug's tail is a barometer of her feelings, so pay close attention to it. Your Pug's tail may wag happily from side to side, uncurling slightly when she is enjoying an exercise. Verbal rewards from you that are high-pitched, excited, and full of energy may produce this response. If her tail uncurls completely, hanging limp or tucked between her legs, she is either confused, frightened, or perhaps too tired to continue a training session.

Happy, confident Pugs have their ears forward and their tail tightly curled.

One of the most difficult tasks when training a Pug is learning how to give a correction without making it come across as too harsh. Many Pugs are quite sensitive to corrections and even the slightest leash or verbal correction may send their tail sagging. These Pugs need a lot of properly timed positive reinforcement in order to teach them and can be a challenge for instructors or owners who do not have a great deal of patience.

You should also watch your Pug's ears and facial expressions. Ears pulled high up on the head in a forward position indicate focus or alertness. If her ears are pulled back your Pug is telling you she is worried or confused about an exercise. Do not correct her when you see that she is confused—this will only make her withdraw from the training session. Try having your Pug perform a behavior she already knows and reward her for it. You should also find a way to break down the exercise you are teaching into smaller, more manageable parts that she can understand.

Pugs thrive on physical contact and positive interaction with their owners. They do not tolerate physical punishment and may become withdrawn or fearful if punishment is used as a way to "teach her who is boss." Pugs that are repeatedly punished quickly learn to try to hide or escape. A Pug who is trying to withdraw from a session will lower her head, pin her ears back, and squint her eyes. Additional withdrawal signals, such as turning away and lowering her body toward the ground, follow. When a Pug withdraws it can be quite difficult to persuade her to continue working, a trait that's earned the breed a reputation for being stubborn and difficult.

Home Schooling

Here are some tips to make sure that your Pug gets the most out of her training sessions:

Keep training sessions short.

Several short sessions each day generally keep your Pug interested in working and allow you to focus on different behaviors if necessary.

Keep training FUN!

Your Pug won't want to work with you if training means you become a drill sergeant.

Be consistent.

Make sure that your rewards and corrections are always timed properly and that your cues are the same each time you ask for a specific behavior.

Encourage proper play.

Exercise is necessary to burn up energy but your Pug needs to learn when it is time to play. A good romp can be a great reward for a training session well done!

Set up a training schedule.

By setting aside a specific time to work with your Pug each day, you will commit yourself to teaching her how to behave properly.

When teaching a new behavior, give a food reward every time the behavior is performed initially.

A bonus food reward is the best way to ensure that your Pug will continue to try to perform. It also ensures that she will believe the behavior is worth it.

Once a behavior is learned, fade the food reward gradually but continue to use a verbal reward (conditioned reinforcer).

You always have your voice with you so don't be afraid to use it to reward for a job well done. Your verbal praise should continue to reward your Pug every time she performs a desired behavior.

Watch for signs of stress or confusion when training.

Excessive panting, licking, or attempts to escape can all signal stress. If you suspect your Pug is worried during a training session, stop what you are working on and go back to a task that she understands so that you can reward her. End on a positive note.

5 *The Well-Equipped Pug*

Training your Pug will be much easier if you have the right tools for the job. Outfitted with the proper training equipment, you will have an easier time communicating with your Pug and will be able to control him effectively. Using the right leash and collar can be the difference in whether he walks nicely along your side or pulls you down the block.

There are a variety of training tools available and knowing what you really need to make training easier can be challenging. Recommendations for collars and leashes can vary considerably even among dog trainers. Some trainers require that you use a specific collar and leash, while others may recommend specific equipment based on your Pug's individual behavior and your training ability. Friends, relatives, and pet store employees may make suggestions based on their past experiences or personal biases. The recommendation of training equipment by others does not guarantee your success.

Choosing a Collar

A proper collar is essential to begin training your Pug. Collars also provide a fun and creative way for you to give your Pug his own identity.

Flat Collars

Nylon or leather flat collars will have a buckle or snap closure making them easy to put on and take off. Flat collars are inexpensive and come in a variety of patterns and colors. Your Pug can express his individuality with a collar for each season, cheer on his favorite sports team, or even don a designer motif for those special occasions.

Your Pug should be properly fitted with a flat collar at all times. If your Pug is under a year of age you will need to check the fit of the collar often to ensure that it does not become too tight. To avoid the possibility of strangulation, never leave a flat collar on your Pug when he is crated.

To find the correct fit simply place a piece of string around your Pug's neck and mark it where it comes together. There should be a small amount of room between the string and the dog's neck. You should be able to comfortably place one or two fingers between your dog's neck and the collar at all times. Adult Pugs or those with excess wrinkles or fat over the back of the neck should be

Training begins with the right collar and leash.

measured between two of the folds for a snug fit.

Measure the length of the string to determine the size of the collar in inches.

You can also take the string to a pet store and use it as a guide for choosing a collar that is the proper size. Ideally the collar should fit with the buckle in the middle hole or with the plastic latch having no more than an inch of excess material.

Training Collars

Just as there are a variety of training methods and styles, the use of training collars can vary greatly between training classes and instructors. Some Pugs are very sensitive to corrections and may learn better when trained using reward-based training while on a flat collar. Other Pugs

may be easily distracted or difficult to motivate. For those Pugs, a training collar may be recommended.

Training collars are tools that have unique designs to help give you better control during training. When used properly these collars can be effective in changing the way your Pug behaves. Training collars allow you to send a signal directly to your Pug that his behavior is wrong, particularly on walks. Training collars are not designed to be left on your Pug like a flat collar and should be

PUG POINTER
Most flat collars allow for two inches in fit. An eighteen-inch collar typically fits a neck sixteen to eighteen inches in circumference.

PUG POINTER

An identification tag is an essential accessory for your Pug's flat collar. When given the chance, Pugs are notorious for visiting the neighborhood. Without some form of identification yours may be mistaken for a stray.

Your Pug's identification tag should include

- Dog's Name
- Your Name
- Your Address
- Current Phone Number
- Alternate Contact or Phone Number

Some city and county governments may also require that an annual dog license or rabies inoculation tag be attached to the collar.

Microchip Identification is a permanent way to positively identify your Pug if he becomes lost without his collar. Using a syringe that is similar to those used to give vaccinations, your veterinarian will insert a small chip under the skin between the shoulder blades. This chip has a unique code which is registered with the manufacturer. Should your Pug wander away from home, shelter personnel and veterinary clinics can use a special scanner to locate the code and trace directly back to you or to your veterinarian.

You will also receive a special tag that alerts others that your Pug has been implanted with the microchip. The tag should be attached to your Pug's flat collar as another form of identification.

A microchip is only a useful identification tool if you complete the registration process. Without your personal information on file with the microchip manufacturer, it could be difficult or impossible to reunite your Pug with your family. This information should be updated if you move or change phone numbers.

reserved for training sessions or for use on walks.

Slip Collar: The slip collar is designed to help control the dog's head. The slip collar is also called a choke collar, but this is really a misnomer. A slip collar should *never* be tightened enough to actually choke your Pug. Slip collars are typically made of chain, but can also be found in leather and nylon. When used correctly the chain slip collar should tighten quickly with an audible "zipper" sound. This sound sends the message that a correction is coming and the dog will feel a tightening on the neck muscles. This double action of auditory and physical correction can be a great tool to quickly change behavior. Nylon and leather slip collars will not produce an auditory signal.

To properly use a slip collar,

1. Take one ring in each hand.
2. Drop the chain through the ring in your right hand. It will now form a loop.
3. Using your left hand, grasp the collar at the bottom of the loop and bring it up and away from your body. It should look like the letter "P." If the collar looks like a backwards "P" it may not

release properly after a correction is given.

4. Place the "P" over your Pug's head and attach the leash. When pulled snug against the neck a slip collar with a proper fit should have no more than two inches of chain between the clasp of the leash and the dog's neck.

5. To give a correction, simply pull on the leash quickly in a "popping" motion. *Do Not* pull and keep the leash tight! A slip collar only works with a quick, firm popping motion, followed by a return to slack in the leash when the correct behavior is exhibited.

6. Repeat the pop-and-release motion as needed.

Your Pug will not experience any unpleasant effects from a slip collar that is used correctly. Damage to the trachea can occur if the slip collar is consistently pulled too tight, or if the dog is allowed to continuously pull against a tightened slip collar.

When used properly, a slip collar can be an effective training collar.

Slip collars were once considered to be the only type of training collar used to change behaviors. Many instructors have moved away from this collar but pet supply stores still recommend them for training. When used correctly they can still be an effective tool.

Prong Collar: A prong collar is also commonly known as a pinch collar. The prong collar applies pressure to the neck muscles when tightened, sending a very distinct physical correction. Prong collars look rather intimidating, but can actually change some behaviors more quickly and effectively than a slip collar. "Kinder" versions of the traditional prong collar are now available: one that has rubber tips over each of the individual prongs and one that is made of plastic instead of the traditional metal.

In an effort to minimize the pressure, which many owners perceive as uncomfortable or painful, prong collars that are too big are often purchased. A properly fitting prong collar should fit snugly on the neck. It should not be loose enough to be able to slide up and down on the neck, nor too tight, applying constant pressure to the muscles. When fitted properly you can simply pull the leash gently to tighten the collar and see a noticeable change in your Pug's behavior.

Prong collars are used exclusively for training classes by some instructors. Other classes will not allow them, and they are prohibited on the show grounds by the American Kennel Club and other organizations. Use of the prong collar can be controversial. Like any other training tool you must be comfortable using it and know how to use it properly.

Electronic Stimulation Collars: Electronic stimulation collars deliver a variable electronic stimulus in response to a signal from a hand-held remote control or in response to a specific stimulus such as barking. Electronic stimulation collars are also called "shock collars." These collars should not be used except under the guidance and supervision of a professional dog trainer. Timing of the corrections delivered to the dog, as well as the proper level of electronic stimulus needed to change the behavior, without causing fear, pain, or anxiety, are critical.

Spray Collars: Spray collars are similar in design to electronic stimulation collars. They deliver a short burst of air or scent, most commonly citronella, in response to a remote control signal or other stimulus. Spray collars can be an effective tool in changing inappropriate barking behavior.

Spray collars are often viewed as a more humane alternative to electronic stimulation collars since there is no electronic "shock" involved. One drawback to using spray collars on Pugs is that their exposed eyes can potentially be irritated by repeated exposure to the spray blasts.

Ultrasonic Collars: Ultrasonic collars use a high-frequency sound to interrupt behaviors. These collars are inexpensive to purchase, but most fail to send a strong enough sound to permanently change unwanted behaviors.

The Harness Dilemma

A harness is a good option for Pugs suffering from tracheal collapse, respiratory conditions, or cervical disc disease, but it is

Make sure that your Pug's collar fits properly.

PUG POINTERS

DO use a training collar for training situations only.

DO use a training collar for changing your Pug's leash walking habits.

DO NOT leave a training collar on your Pug when he is unattended, on a tie out, or on a retractable leash.

DO NOT leave a training collar on a crated dog.

DO NOT use a slip collar if your Pug suffers from tracheal collapse or cervical disc disease.

a poor choice for a training tool. A harness distributes any signal from a leash correction over the shoulders. The sensation of a correction is distributed over a wider area, providing poor control and allowing your Pug to pull on walks as effectively as a sled dog!

Many owners who have not taught their Pugs to properly walk on a leash feel sorry for them when they cough or gag due to the constant collar pressure created by the pulling behavior. Instead of using a training collar and dedicating time to teaching their Pug how to walk properly, they switch to a harness. These Pugs never learn how to properly walk on a leash and continue to pull (often times worse than ever). The owners, however, feel better because they no longer hear their Pug gagging or choking when they are on leash. It's kinder to teach your Pug to walk properly in the first place.

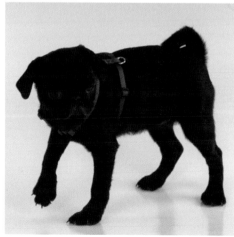

It can be difficult to train your Pug when he wears a harness.

Leash on Life

The proper leash can also be the difference in not only whether your Pug learns to walk properly with you, but also in how comfortable the walk is for you. Leashes are available in a variety of types and lengths, but they are not all used for the same purpose.

Your everyday leash can be a nylon lead in a pattern or color to match your Pug's flat collar, or a soft, leather lead. A length of four feet is generally enough to allow the dog to walk comfortably near you. Too much more will allow your Pug to pull ahead and potentially get into trouble. A wide leash is often more difficult to grasp than a narrow style. Nylon leashes tend to be stiffer and more uncomfortable to work with in colder climates, especially if you are taking a walk without gloves. Corrections given with a nylon leash may give you a slight sting in the palm of your hand. Leather leads can be used comfortably in most weather conditions.

Training Leashes

A leather leash is an excellent choice for a training leash and can double as your everyday leash too. Leather is lightweight and very easy on your hands. Leather leashes can be more expensive than nylon leashes, but usually last for years.

Your training leash should be six feet in length. This length allows you to work with your Pug at a short distance without giving him too much freedom.

Chain leashes are a poor choice as they are bulky and difficult to hold on to com-

fortably. Still, many owners feel that a chain leash is necessary when their Pug has repeatedly chewed through nylon or leather leashes. If your Pug chews on his leash, he should be taught not to do so instead of changing to an "indestructible" lead. Changing to a chain leash only allows him the opportunity to continue the wrong behavior, instead of teaching him that the leash is off limits to teeth.

Specialty Leashes: Leashes that are longer than the traditional four and six foot leads have special uses in training. Retractable leads are great for teaching your Pug behaviors at a distance without having to worry about him leaving the training session early. Many people try to

Sitting and staying can be made easier with the right training tools.

use them for their everyday leash as well. Retractable leashes are a poor choice for an everyday leash for the following reasons:

1. The further your Pug is from you the less control you have.
2. Corrections take longer to reach the dog and have minimal or no impact when they do reach.

51

A slip lead is a leash and a collar all in one.

3. Situations may occur where your Pug needs to be immediately under control or injury may result. These include encounters with unfriendly dogs, dogs that are off leash, ingesting objects while on walks, or the sudden appearance of vehicles.
4. Rapid retraction of these leads can cause injuries to both you and your Pug.

Retractable leashes can be used to give more space for elimination when you are in an area that is not secure. If you must walk your Pug on a retractable leash remember to keep it locked at a distance that is short, preferably four feet.

Long lines, or web training leads, come in lengths from ten to fifty feet. The purpose of these leashes is to allow the dog to move to a distance away from you for teaching exercises such as *come*, while still giving you a way to communicate.

Training Treats

Training treats are another tool to use when working with your Pug. Most Pugs are highly motivated by food, making the task of finding treats that your Pug will be willing to work for quite easy.

Experiment with a variety of food rewards to determine those your Pug likes best. Each food reward will have a value to your Pug based on how interesting it smells and tastes. This value partially determines whether or not your Pug can be motivated to learn or perform any behavior.

Let's say, for example, you want your Pug to perform the *sit* command. At home, where distractions are minimal, your Pug will gladly sit quickly for a dog biscuit, pieces of dry dog food, or small pieces of cereal. The treat has high enough value for him to work for you in an environment

A long leash is used for training your Pug at a distance.

Leash and Learn

When you ask your Pug to go for a walk does he get excited, jumping at you in anticipation? Before you can begin to teach him how to walk properly on a leash, you must know how to use the leash effectively to communicate your message. Holding the leash correctly, timing your signal to send the message that a behavior is right or wrong, and teaching your Pug where you want him on walks should all be part of the leash training process.

Please remember that any leash corrections should be just enough to get your Pug's attention—not hard enough to move him off of his feet. Praise and reward may work better to change some behaviors than constant corrections for most Pugs. Loose-lead heeling takes time and effort; you cannot expect change overnight. It is most important to reward for the behavior you want.

that he is comfortable in. If your children come home or a visitor enters the room, your Pug may no longer sit as quickly for the same reward. The possibility of an interaction with the kids or your guest is now his priority. In order for his response to be as quick, you need to provide something higher in value to work for. A piece of hot dog, lunch meat, or cheese may be needed to bring your Pug's attention back to you and the *sit*. The more distractions that your Pug is exposed to, the greater the value of the reward needs to be.

You can also think of training treats as Pug currency. What food reward does your Pug consider to be one dollar, ten dollars, or one hundred dollars? Is the behavior you are teaching worth the same amount or is there some other reward that your Pug believes is worth more? Training treats do not have to be only food, although most Pugs prefer eating to anything else! A favorite toy can be substituted for food rewards as long as it is high enough in value.

Training will be a snap if you find different food rewards that your Pug is willing to work for.

Home Schooling

Teaching Heel *Position*

Heel position is the location you want your Pug to be in at all times when he is on leash. The universally accepted *heel* position is on your left side, with your Pug's shoulder directly in line with your leg. When the dog is in the proper position the leash will be loose.

To teach your Pug where *heel* position is, you will need to reward him whenever he is in the correct location. It is best to begin with the leash held comfortably in your right hand. Gather up approximately one to two feet of the leash in your right hand, allowing the remaining length of the leash to fall in front of you with enough slack to form a fish hook connecting the dog to you. Place a treat in your left hand and allow it to hang loosely along your left leg. Get your Pug's attention by saying his name and wiggle your fingers to draw him toward *heel* position. As soon as he is in *heel* position, verbally reward him with a "*good boy,*" bend at the knees and let him take the treat from your fingers. Do not turn to face him. You want him to learn that *heel* position is next to you, not in front of you.

Once your Pug is good at finding *heel* position when you are stationary, you can put some movement into this exercise. As he moves into *heel* position, walk away and turn slightly to your right. You can use his name to get his attention and wiggle your fingers to help lure him to *heel* position, but do not turn to look at him or stop and wait for him. Each time he finds it, verbally reward and provide a food reward.

If your Pug moves around to your right side instead of the left you probably made too sharp of a turn or didn't have enough of a visual cue (your left hand was not easily visible). Try placing your left hand a bit more behind you and make certain that you wiggle those fingers!

Now let's get the dog's focus! Instead of placing your left hand along your left leg, bring it up toward your left hip. This should pull your Pug's focus up toward your face. As soon as he looks up, verbally reward him and then give the food reward. Your Pug should rapidly begin to realize that being on your left side and looking up to you produces a verbal reward and a treat. Once your Pug has learned to walk on your left side, focusing on your left hip, it is time to begin delaying the food reward and increasing your movement. Make sure that you immediately reward him verbally when in heel position, but continue moving in a forward direction for a few steps before you give the food reward.

Your Pug must learn to *heel* in a straight line without any distractions, before you can ever expect him to walk nicely with you on

Teaching your Pug to *heel* takes time and effort.

walks. You should progress from finding *heel* position to moving forward in *heel* position a few steps while maintaining focus on you. If your Pug is unable to maintain focus for just a few steps, go back to rewarding *heel* position with just a turn and try again. Maintaining attention is very important, as focus is one of the keys to loose-lead heeling.

Once your Pug can *heel* for three or four steps forward, try lengthening the number of steps you take before you verbally reward and treat. Do not try to jump from three or four steps to twenty! Increase your steps gradually, rewarding your Pug when he is focused and in *heel* position.

In the beginning, use your voice to help keep your Pug focused as you move forward. Enthusiastic praise can motivate the dog to move while still paying attention to you. Don't forget to tell him "good boy" before you give the treat! Once he has mastered straight-line heeling without distractions, it is time to begin working outside.

Loose Lead Heeling

The keys to teaching the *heel* on a loose lead with distractions are the following:

- Rewarding focus
- Correcting for improper position
- Rewarding for finding/maintaining proper position

If your Pug cannot stay focused and does not know *heel* position, he cannot be expected to heel on a loose lead. Don't skimp on teaching how to find *heel* position first! Begin in *heel* position. Say the dog's name, give the *heel* command, and step forward with your left leg briskly.

If your Pug remains in *heel* position and is focused: Praise him with enthusiasm and continue forward a short distance, verbally reward him, and give a treat. Repeat this exercise many times, continuing to reward for heeling short distances. This part of the learning process is very important. Most Pugs learn more quickly when they are rewarded for good behavior. Spending a considerable amount of time rewarding straight line heeling means that you will have to correct less when you begin going longer distances. Over time, begin to increase the distance you move forward before you reward and treat.

If your Pug bolts forward in front of you: Move backwards quickly and use your leash to simultaneously pop towards you. Your Pug should turn and begin to move in your direction. Praise him and encourage him to find *heel* position and try again.

If your Pug remains behind you: Turn to face your Pug and verbally encourage him to catch up and find *heel* position again. You can move backwards and use your leash to pop towards you. Do not use harsh leash corrections. This may make the dog confused or hesitant to move. Try a slight pop to motivate him to move forward.

If your Pug looks away from you as soon as you start moving forward: First ask yourself "Did I really have my Pug's attention before I started?" If you didn't, you might need to work harder on teaching him to move forward while focused. Next try rewarding his focus before you start moving by saying his name and watching for him to look up at you. When he does IMMEDIATELY reward him with a "good boy" followed by a treat or two for a bonus. Then try to repeat the exercise.

If your Pug moves too far to the left or looks away while you are moving: Turn to face the dog. Begin to move away backwards and encourage him to find *heel* position again. Reward him when he does. Repeat the exercise.

You should practice teaching your Pug how to *heel* on a loose lead for a short distance before you ever try to take him for a walk around the block. Fifteen minutes spent each day in your driveway, rewarding him for proper position and correcting him when he is out of position, will teach him what you expect when you go for a walk.

Heeling Distractions and Complications

As your Pug learns to keep up with you, focused and relaxed heeling with added distractions should be your goal. Here are some common situations and how to work through them.

Sniffing: Your Pug isn't focused enough on you! Go back to rewarding attentive behavior or try to gain attention using your voice or a food lure and reward as soon as he gives you his attention. You can also use the *leave it* command outlined in Chapter 7.

Lunging ahead: A common mistake if your Pug sees something he is interested in. Once again we have a focus issue. Try turning away from the direction your Pug wants to go by doing an about turn, or a 180-degree turn to your right. Be aware of when the dog finds *heel* position and reward immediately.

Crowding (heeling too close to you): Try bumping your Pug away from

you with your left leg as you turn 90 degrees into him and keep walking. You can also turn 180 degrees to the left (a U-turn) and reward him for finding *heel* position again.

Stopping: Your Pug may want to stop to observe the world around him but he doesn't have to. If he stops suddenly give him a quick pop forward with the leash and be ready to reward him as soon as he finds *heel* position. If you think your Pug may have stopped in response to being frightened by something, finding *heel* position and getting both a verbal "good boy" followed by a couple of treats will help him realize that *heel* position is a great place to be.

If you stop and wait for your Pug to go again, he will quickly realize that his actions can control yours. Do not give into him if he stops. Keep him moving and be sure to reward him for doing so.

Marking behaviors: Pugs of both sexes may be driven to stop and mark instead of heeling nicely on a loose lead. Once again, your Pug doesn't HAVE to mark fifty times on a walk but will if you allow him to. Change this behavior by treating it as stopping or lunging (see above).

Going for a walk with your Pug on a loose lead, quietly trotting along your side, can be a relaxing way to spend time together. There are no shortcuts to teaching him how to walk properly. Use the proper techniques outlined above and combine them with the right collar and leash for your Pug's age and temperament. Dedicate your time and energy to training how to *heel* correctly.

6 Housebreaking and Confinement Training

The most frequent complaint you will hear from Pug owners is how difficult it was to housebreak their Pug. A Pug should be no more difficult to housetrain than a Labrador Retriever or a German Shepherd. To ensure your Pug's success you must be committed to completing the entire training process correctly.

The Golden Rule

By definition a Pug is considered to be housebroken when she has successfully remained clean with *no* accidents for a full eight weeks. This will only happen with constant supervision from you, combined with confinement to a properly sized area when supervision is impractical or impossible. This process will take months to complete, and in many cases may take a full year or more. Do not make excuses for your Pug! The majority of owners who complain about their Pugs' housebreaking failures were not committed to seeing the job done right and failed to supervise or confine properly.

Factors Affecting Housebreaking

Successfully housebreaking your Pug should be a family goal. Everyone must be involved with the training process in order for it to be easy and successful. Many factors influence housebreaking, especially during puppyhood. Understanding these factors, and learning to predict when your Pug will have to eliminate based on her daily routine, will make housetraining easier on both of you. Your daily routine will have to be a bit flexible at first in order to help your Pug understand the concept.

Sleep

Rest patterns, or periods of sleep and inactivity, directly affect a dog's need to urinate. The first person to wake up each morning must immediately give your Pug the opportunity to urinate in an appropriate location. If she has been taking a well-deserved nap during a busy day, she will also need the opportunity to urinate as

When naptime is over it is time to go potty.

soon as she wakes up. With Pug puppies, urination will happen within one to three minutes following any period of rest.

Nutrition

Mealtime also has a direct relationship with housebreaking. As soon as a meal is consumed the intestinal tract springs to life. A Pug puppy will generally have a bowel movement within minutes after she eats, while an adult Pug may have slower results. If you feed three meals per day, as is often the case with puppies, you can then expect to have a minimum of three potty trips for "doody duty." Most puppies will also give you at least one "bonus" each day! Adult Pugs fed once each day may only need one or two potty trips.

If feeding is "free choice," or food is available at all times, housebreaking may be quite difficult. The opportunity to eat whenever your Pug wants, in any quantity she wants, leads to an intestinal tract in a constant state of motion. Constant motility leads to bowel movements at unpredictable times throughout the day and night. Feeding a specific number of meals and a measured amount of food can help establish a more predictable outcome.

The type of food provided also factors into housetraining. Quality dog foods, made from premium ingredients with minimal fillers, are easier to digest. With better digestion you get smaller volume of stool, resulting in fewer trips to go potty! Pugs fed only canned or soft, moist food may have to urinate more frequently due to the increased water and sugar contents of these diets.

Your Pug's water intake also affects how often she'll need to eliminate. If she

Your Pug's mealtime also affects potty time.

drinks a large amount of water at any one time, she'll need a potty trip soon after. When housebreaking a Pug puppy, it is a good idea not to allow your puppy to drink a lot of water in the late evening. A good rule of thumb is to allow access to water for one to two hours past her evening meal and restrict water consumption thereafter. Exceptions can be made following an evening walk, during hot weather, or after any other activity that may make her hot or thirsty. Ice cubes can make a wonderful treat in the evening, satisfying the need for water and providing your Pug with something fun to eat.

Metabolism

Perhaps the most misunderstood factor in housebreaking a Pug is her metabolism, or

surges in her activity level. Anytime your Pug's metabolism increases, she produces urine. Puppies are particularly susceptible to having accidents caused by normal puppy activity. Many owners cannot understand why their Pug has an accident ten to fifteen minutes after she has just urinated in an appropriate location. They fail to realize that normal activity, such as playing with toys, can cause the need to urinate again very quickly. Unless you constantly monitor your Pug's activity, especially as a puppy, you may miss the opportunity to help her eliminate in an appropriate place.

Some of the more common activities that result in metabolism surges are:

■ **Playtime behaviors.** Playing with toys, people, or other pets causes an increase in metabolism.

- **Running or taking a walk.** Running throughout the house, or simply following you from room to room can be enough to increase metabolism.
- **Periods of excitement.** Children arriving home from school, the doorbell indicating a visitor, even the phone ringing can all trigger metabolism surges.
- **Periods of anxiety.** Loud noises, thunderstorms, even strangers can be scary!
- **Episodes of barking.** Barking indicates excitement, anxiety, arousal, or fear.

Housebreaking 101

Housebreaking is a partnership. You and your Pug must work as a team in order for her to understand what it is you want her to do, and more importantly, where

Periods of playful activity mean that your Pug will need to eliminate soon.

you want her to do it. Contrary to what most people believe, successful housebreaking is 90 percent owner responsibility, observation, and timing and 10 percent Pug stool, urine production, and the need to eliminate. A Pug puppy's schedule will change as she matures. As a puppy gets older, her bladder control improves and her need to eliminate is stretched out over longer periods of time. She can then successfully go several hours without having to take a potty break. Young Pug puppies require frequent *successful* trips to a chosen spot before the concept of housebreaking can begin to take shape. Adult Pugs experiencing frequent or continuous lapses of housebreaking should be treated as if they were still a puppy.

You will need to create a routine that is followed by everyone in your household in order to begin the housebreaking process.

Choose a Potty Spot

You cannot begin to start housetraining your Pug until you decide where it is you want her to eliminate. It is best to choose a location that is outdoors, but with access close enough to be convenient when you are in a hurry. Try to choose a spot near the main area where your puppy will be kept. One way to help your Pug learn the location of her potty spot is to use the same door every time you take him outside.

Choose a Potty Word

Create a word or phrase that tells your Pug what you want her to do, and make sure that every family member uses the same word or phrase. As soon as you take your puppy to her potty spot, a simple command such as *"go potty"* or *"do a job"* should be given on a frequent basis. If you are consistent and use the same words, over time they will become a cue for your puppy to eliminate on command. Your voice can also be used to help stimulate your Pug to complete the task at hand. By saying your word or phrase in a high-pitched, excited voice you will excite the dog, increasing her metabolism and helping to quickly get her to eliminate.

As puppies get more confident, they often get a bit more interested in what is going on around them. If your Pug seems preoccupied with things other than going potty, walk a short distance away from her and call her to follow you. Remember that the simple activity of walking stimulates the urge to eliminate.

Reward Your Pug's Success

As soon as your puppy begins to eliminate in the correct location, verbally praise her. By rewarding her with an excited, happy *"good potty"* or *"good job"* you'll send the message that you are pleased with her behavior. If your Pug stops eliminating at the sound of your voice, immediately stop your verbal praise. Wait until she begins to urinate again and try praising her again in a tone of voice that is slightly quieter and somewhat less excited.

A small food reward may be given as a bonus when the dog is finished with her job. This food reward should be timed so that it is given at the spot in which she eliminated and not when you return inside

Successful housebreaking takes considerable time and effort.

the house. A food reward given once she returns inside rewards entering the house, not the successful elimination outside minutes earlier. An appropriately timed food reward eliminates the possibility that your Pug will learn to run outside, turn around and return to the house to get her treat, without successfully eliminating first.

Do not be in a hurry to stop verbally rewarding your Pug for eliminating in the right spot. Rewards are the only way to ensure that a behavior is truly learned, and by actually seeing your Pug eliminate, you'll know that the task has been successfully completed.

Interrupt Mistakes

If you catch your Pug making a potty "mistake," you need to interrupt her

Verbally praise your Pug when she eliminates in the correct location.

immediately. Startle her by clapping your hands or making a loud noise, and then immediately take her to the potty spot. Give her a chance to finish eliminating in the right place and then praise her for doing so, as if the accident never occurred. You can give yourself a little praise too, for supervising her and catching the accident as it occurred.

If you find a mistake after it has occurred, you didn't follow the Golden Rule; you and your puppy were not a team and you were not effectively supervising your Pug. Don't bring your Pug to the accident to show her her mistake—doing so won't aid in the housetraining

process. It may make you feel better, but to your Pug it creates confusion. If you storm up to her, speaking in a tone of voice full of disapproval, she will believe that whatever behavior she is doing at that moment is bad. She won't know that she was "bad" because she eliminated in the house minutes or hours ago. Instead she will read your body language and your vocal tones and believe that you are displeased with her for whatever she is involved in at that time.

Clean Up Correctly

The reality of owning a Pug is that accidents will occur during the housebreaking process. You need to be prepared to deal with them by having the right products on hand to make cleanup easy, minimize any residual odors, and decrease stains.

Dogs use their sense of smell to pick their potty spot. Ammonia is one of many components found in dog urine and it is believed to be one reason why dogs will return to the same area repeatedly to urinate. While this is great for training your Pug to eliminate at the chosen spot, accidents indoors must be quickly and completely cleaned and deodorized.

Many products available through pet supply retailers, catalogs, and veterinary clinics use natural enzymes to break down urine odors. Follow the specific directions on the label, and make sure that your Pug is not allowed access to the area until it is completely dry. Some locations, such as thick carpeting, may require more than one application before the odor is completely eliminated. A vinegar and water solution can also be used in a pinch, but it does not have the complete breakdown capabilities of specialized pet odor and stain removers.

Potty Time, Not Playtime

Some Pugs prefer to explore their environment, especially if their potty spot is outdoors. It is important for your Pug to learn that potty time is very different from playtime. Your interactions with your Pug during potty time should reflect this as well. Whenever you are at the potty spot, you should refrain from playing games. Remind your Pug that she is outside for a specific purpose by remaining still and using the potty word. Do not engage in play behaviors or reward for any behavior other than a successful potty trip.

Some adult Pugs, as well as some Pugs that are just reaching maturity, may require a bit more time to complete their job. They really aren't interested in playing or exploring, they are simply letting their sense of smell determine exactly where elimination should occur. These Pugs become very choosy about where they wish to eliminate, and cannot be rushed into making a decision.

Supervise Your Pug

Lack of proper supervision is all too often the reason Pugs fail to become completely housetrained. Most owners supervise effectively when they first bring their Pug home as a puppy, but fail to continue this step as she matures. Effective supervision means that someone is watching your Pug at all times. Distractions such as

Don't take a vacation from your Pug's house-breaking!

phone calls, working on the computer, or watching television give your Pug ample time to sneak away and have an accident without you knowing it has occurred.

Proper supervision also gives you the opportunity to learn about your Pug's pattern of behavior before she eliminates. Very few Pugs ever learn to bark as a signal before they need to "go." Pug puppies generally give very subtle signals that elimination is inevitable, and it is up to you to learn to recognize them. Your puppy may begin to sniff the floor, circle in place, or simply pace back and forth for a few moments before urinating. As she gets older, she may learn to head toward the door that has given her access to her potty spot. Each Pug is unique in how she signals that she needs to eliminate. Keen observation while supervising your Pug is the only way you will learn to recognize her signals.

Confine Your Pug

When you are unable to devote 100 percent of your attention to supervising your puppy she should be confined to an appropriate area. Confinement is not punishment and is not to be used after an accident has occurred to "make a point."

It is simply a way to safely keep your Pug out of harm's way and an effective tool to prevent her from choosing one or more indoor locations for potty spots.

Confinement Training

Confinement training, also called crate training, operates on the theory that, like wolves and other wild dogs, domestic dogs seek comfort in a secure den-like area. A crate can quickly become that "den"—a safe and secure place for your Pug to call home.

Most Pugs are generally clean and do not want to eliminate in the living space where they sleep and eat. The goal is for the crate to become your Pug's living space. Spending time in the crate should not be viewed as a bad thing. A properly crate-trained Pug will happily enter her crate on her own or on your command, and will rest quietly whether you are home or away.

Remember that confinement training and housebreaking go hand in hand. It is very difficult to have a housebroken Pug when no form of confinement training is being practiced. Purchasing the right crate for your Pug is an essential part of housetraining.

Creating a Living Space

Feeding your Pug in her crate is a great way to make the crate inviting. If she sleeps in her crate and has her meals delivered to her there, she is less likely to eliminate in the same space.

Any form of soft, washable bedding can be used in the crate to make your Pug's new living space more comfortable. Pug puppies seem to prefer artificial sheepskin rugs, thick towels, or baby blankets. These items are easily washable should your puppy have an unexpected accident. Puppies may also chew on their bedding, so it is best to choose a bedding material that is inexpensive to replace. Adult Pugs are less likely to chew inappropriately on their bedding, making a thick foam bed or pillow an excellent addition to the crate.

The location of the crate is up to you. It's best to situate it in an area that is close enough for you to hear your Pug should she whine as a signal that she needs a potty break, especially if you have a puppy. Select a location that is out of direct sunlight during the day—you don't want your Pug to get too warm while you are away. A location that does not offer a lot of distractions should also be considered. If the crate is near a glass door or window, where the sights and sounds of people, cars, and other dogs may be nearly constant, your Pug will spend less time resting and more time in a state of activity. Remember that increased activity means increased metabolism—and the need to eliminate more frequently.

Many Pug owners choose to keep crates in multiple locations. Placing a crate on each level of your home offers you the flexibility to properly confine your Pug when you cannot watch her, no matter where you are in your house. Have your Pug spend a small amount of time in each crate so that she gets comfortable with each location. Moving your Pug's crate from one area of the house to another

Your Pug's crate will become his or her "Home Sweet Home."

can also be an option, but this may confuse for your Pug. If she is tired and looking for her crate, and can't find it in its usual location, she may become slightly anxious. Anxiety, even in small amounts, can increase the need to eliminate.

Mobile Home: Your pug's crate can be taken with you when you travel. Traveling can be stressful and having her own space in an unfamiliar location can help ease your Pug's anxiety and make travel more pleasant. Many hotels now require canine guests to be confined while they stay, and relatives who may not otherwise allow your Pug to visit may be more hospitable if she is comfortable being crated.

Travel by car is also much safer for a Pug confined to a crate. Your Pug will learn to quietly ride in her home, leaving you to concentrate on driving safely. In the event of an accident your Pug is less likely to suffer severe injuries when crated. Riding

Crates are a safe way for your Pug to travel.

loose in the car she could be injured when an air bag deploys. She could be thrown from the vehicle, or escape when rescue personnel try to help on your behalf.

Crate Sizes and Types: Dog crates or kennels come in a variety of styles, sizes, and colors. The style you choose is a matter of personal preference rather than function. Both wire and plastic airline-type crates are suitable homes for a Pug. Many wire crates fold easily making them very portable. Wire crates also offer better ventilation in warmer climates. Plastic kennels give a Pug a more enclosed feeling and may benefit Pugs who prefer a more private sleeping area.

The size of your crate is very important. While you might want to give your Pug as much space as possible, purchasing a crate that is too big may actually hinder the housetraining process. The crate should offer enough space to stand up comfortably, turn around easily, and lie down. If you have a puppy, wire crates with movable dividers offer the flexibility to increase crate space as she grows. A crate that is too big from the start allows your Pug the option of eliminating at one end, and sleeping comfortably at the other. Remember that the goal is to provide a clean and dry space to sleep, not to supply enough space to eliminate and then go to sleep. When confined to a crate, a Pug who is properly confinement trained will let her owner know when she has to eliminate.

Let's Go "Bedtime"

Get your Pug accustomed to voluntarily entering her crate. When she eagerly runs into her crate on your command, it makes confinement training a breeze. You should begin to work toward this goal from the first day you bring your new Pug home.

To begin confinement training, choose a word that will be used to tell your puppy to enter her crate. *"Bedtime"* or *"go to bed"* should be used every time you want her to go into her crate. If you are feeding in the crate, that is *"bedtime"* too. Anytime your Pug is asked to go into her crate you will use the same phrase, and you must then reward her for the right behavior—entering the crate on her own.

To teach her this behavior, start crate training as a game. In the beginning, her reward can be a small yummy treat. Show the treat to your Pug and when she is interested and following it, toss it into the crate. As she begins to follows it into the crate, reward her with a *"good bedtime."* The food reward will eventually become a bonus. Once she understands the game, you can add your bedtime word or phrase just before you toss the food reward into the crate. You should practice this at least several times each day, independently from the times you actually need to put her into the crate. When you do need to put her in her crate for confinement, follow the same procedure and don't forget the food reward! Many Pug breeders continue to reward this behavior every time, even when their Pugs are older. If you con-

sistently reward your Pug for entering her crate voluntarily, she will be running into her crate at your request in no time at all.

Most Pugs adapt to crate training very quickly. When yours makes a beeline for her crate on your command, you can then begin to reward her after she enters the crate instead of tossing the reward in ahead of her. The more you reward, the faster she will learn this behavior.

Some Pugs, especially during their adolescence, may try to outsmart owners by refusing to enter the crate. This behavior usually begins when an owner fails to give an appropriate food reward, or has stopped rewarding altogether. Most Pugs are highly motivated by food. Try changing your food reward to something a bit more enticing on occasion, and you'll keep your Pug eager for a chance to go *"bedtime."*

In review, the crate training sequence should become

1. Give the verbal command, *"bedtime."*
2. Your Pug enters the crate voluntarily.
3. Reward with *"good bedtime."*
4. Toss the food reward into the crate.

Remember that this sequence should be used every time you want your Pug to enter her crate. Once she has learned and perfected this behavior, the reward you use can be her dinner, a treat, or a special toy. Anything that your Pug considers of value and motivates her can be used as a reward.

Crate Alternatives

During the day, the crate should be used whenever you need to confine your Pug for a short duration of time, say four to five hours or less. However, since many Pug owners work full time, or plan to be gone for longer periods of time, a conflict arises between providing safe confinement and the need for your Pug to be able to move around during her daytime periods of activity. Puppies less than six months of age cannot realistically be expected not to urinate for longer than a few hours during the day. An alternative confinement space, one that provides enough room for your Pug to sleep, room to play with toys, and has an acceptable indoor potty spot if necessary, should be considered.

For adult Pugs with no issues with separation anxiety and no destructive tendencies, a utility room, hallway, or bathroom can be turned into a suitable daytime play area. Place a comfortable bed in the area, give your Pug some interactive, rewarding toys, and leave quietly

with a pleasant "goodbye," and you've established a wonderful daytime living space for an adult Pug. Use baby gates to create doorway barriers. Leaving your Pug in a room with the doors closed can make her feel isolated. Isolation can create anxiety, which can lead to attempts to escape from the area. The result is an owner who comes home to find his doorway and walls scratched by a frantic Pug. Increased anxiety about your departure may follow, and inappropriate elimination may occur because of your Pug's anxious state of mind.

Pug puppies require a slightly different approach to their accommodations. The area must be safe from curious puppy teeth, easy for you to clean, and free from dangers that your puppy may be interested in exploring. A safe environment can be provided by purchasing a puppy play yard or exercise pen and using it with your puppy's crate.

To create a puppy daytime play space, attach the exercise pen to the sides of the puppy's wire crate. If you have a plastic airline crate, simply place the crate inside the enclosed pen. The crate door should be left open to allow him access to her "bedtime" spot. Newspaper or puppy housetraining pads can be placed in the pen on the side opposite her crate. This indoor potty spot should be as far away from her crate as possible. A small bowl of water, either attached to the side of the pen, or heavy enough so that it is difficult to spill, should be available during the day. Give your Pug a few toys that reward her for playing with them. Toys that drop small food rewards will keep her busy for longer periods of time than plush toys or chew bones.

Outdoor dog runs or fenced enclosures are not suitable confinement alternatives for Pugs. Pugs should never be left outdoors when unsupervised or for long periods of time. The breed is very vulnerable to heat and cold and exposure to temperature extremes for even short periods of time can be fatal. Pug eyes are prone to injury, and their inquisitive nature often has them poking around the bushes to flush out birds, chipmunks, and rabbits. Pugs are also prone to anaphylactic reactions to insect stings and bites, making a simple bee sting potentially deadly as well. Many Pugs are also very determined excavators and an outdoor enclosure is no match for these explorers!

Pugs left outside unattended may be quickly taken from their enclosure. The theft and resale of small dogs, particularly breeds that are as popular as the Pug, is an unfortunate trend in many areas. Pug puppies left outside unattended are small enough to be snatched by birds of prey in many areas, or taken by a hungry coyote or fox.

Overnight Accommodations

Nighttime for a Pug should be a period of prolonged rest and minimal activity. During periods of rest, the body is producing urine, but until the bladder reaches its capacity, the urge to eliminate is minimal. The last person in the household to go to sleep each evening should be responsible for giving your Pug one last trip to the potty spot.

A puppy may need the opportunity to visit the potty spot once during the night.

Never leave your Pug outside unattended.

An eight-to-nine-week-old puppy usually has the capability and the bladder capacity to remain clean for no more than four hours when she is in a period of rest. That means that you will have to set your alarm for four hours after she goes to bed, or, if you are a light sleeper, hope that your puppy whines, cries, or barks prior to urinating in her crate—and that you hear her in time to get her to the potty spot. As your Pug gets older, her bladder capacity will increase and the time she can remain clean will increase as well. A good guide to follow is

- 8 to 9 weeks of age—4 hours at night
- 10 to 12 weeks of age—5 hours at night
- 13 to 15 weeks of age—6 hours at night

- 16 weeks of age and older—7 to 8 hours at night

Remember that these are guidelines. Your puppy's progress may be slightly faster or slower.

By four months of age, most Pug puppies are able to give you a full eight hours of sleep each night. Because housetraining a Pug is a family affair, one way to avoid sleep deprivation during those early weeks is to take turns getting up with a puppy. Older children can be given the responsibility on weekends, and parents should share the duty during the week.

If it is impossible for you to take your Pug to her potty spot during the overnight hours, do not force her to eliminate in her crate. This creates confusion and will have an impact in her willingness to stay clean in her crate during the day. A better solution is to give her an alternative confinement space, one with an indoor potty spot where she can eliminate away from the crate. If this method is chosen, housebreaking may take a bit longer. Allowing a puppy free access to eliminate overnight does not help teach bladder or bowel control, and does not help to strengthen or stretch the bladder.

Indoor Potty Spots

Indoor potty spots are commonly used by individuals that live in high-rise apartment buildings, those who cannot access the outdoors quickly, or by owners who live in climates with cold winter months.

Pugs can be taught to eliminate on a specific substrate indoors. Many Pugs actually prefer newspapers or puppy pads, having learned to use this substrate as puppies. Many Pugs have been successfully trained to eliminate in a litter box filled with wood shavings or clay litter. Before you consider using an indoor potty spot, you should be aware of the problems that commonly occur when using these locations.

The success of this alternative method depends greatly on you and how diligent you are in supervising your Pug. Remember that most Pugs do not wish to eliminate in their living space. An indoor potty spot may decrease or eliminate this aversion, making your entire home an acceptable option to some Pugs. Most Pugs do not distinguish the difference between newspapers or potty pads on the floor and an oriental rug. To the Pug who has to eliminate, anything that is rectangular and on the floor seems like an acceptable option.

Male Pugs who lift their legs to urinate will need to have an acceptable, vertical object at the indoor potty spot. Once again, supervision will be needed at all times in order to ensure that he does not find another vertical location indoors that he prefers. Furniture legs are particularly inviting, as are curtains.

If your Pug is already used to eliminating indoors she can be taught to eliminate outside. You will need to eliminate access to the previous indoor area completely and provide her with the same substrate in the new outdoor location. Newspapers can be weighted down outdoors or an area of wood shavings can be created in an outdoor location. You will need to follow all of the rules in Housebreaking 101 (page 60), and make sure that she is supervised outdoors at all times.

Inappropriate Elimination

Although some will not admit it, inappropriate elimination is a problem that many Pug owners live with on a regular basis. Pugs seem unusually prone to lapses in housebreaking. Some of these lapses happen frequently; others are infrequent. Whenever a Pug eliminates in a spot other than the correct potty spot location, she is displaying inappropriate elimination. The reasons for the mistakes vary with each dog, but can generally be broken down into specific causes. Once a cause or causes can be determined, steps can be taken to prevent inappropriate elimination from occurring.

One way to prevent inappropriate elimination from becoming a problem is to keep a log of your Pug's daily potty habits for several weeks or months. Each day, track the approximate time of elimination, and where it occurred. You may begin to see a pattern develop where accidents occur only during specific periods of time, or only in certain areas. Once you see the pattern, you can begin to look for the specific cause or causes.

- Are accidents occurring right after the school bus arrives? Increased activity may be the problem or perhaps supervision is impossible when the children arrive home and report on their day.
- Are accidents occurring only on the rugs? Your Pug may have a preference for carpet or may think it is a potty pad or newspaper.
- Are accidents occurring in one room or on one person's belongings? Your Pug

may be exhibiting marking behavior or have a location preference.
- Do accidents occur only when the weather is inclement? Many Pugs hate to get their feet wet or do not enjoy cold weather. She may need more frequent trips outside.
- Do accidents occur only when one family member is responsible for supervising? Is he or she really supervising?
- Are the accidents always urine, stool, or both? Accidents that are only one elimination or the other may signal a medical condition.

Incomplete Housetraining

Incomplete housetraining is the most common cause of housebreaking lapses in toy breeds, including the Pug. Many owners give their Pug puppy too much freedom to roam within their homes too quickly, and never really fully supervise them. These puppies often have accidents out of the owner's sight, and never complete a full eight to twelve weeks without accidents. The owner is unaware that the accidents have been occurring all on a regular basis. As the Pug matures, the owner often begins to take notice as the size of the accidents increase, the urine becomes more concentrated, and staining of the Pug's favorite potty areas begins to occur. The now young adult Pug has no aversion to eliminating near the owner because he considers the entire house an acceptable indoor potty spot. After all, she has been eliminating in the house for a long time, and her owner never gave

Newspaper can be placed inside a puppy's exercise pen for an indoor potty spot.

her any indication that it was either a positive behavior or a negative behavior.

The majority of adult Pugs that are available in rescue programs are there, solely or in part, because they are incompletely housetrained. It is important to remember that these Pugs have never completely understood that eliminating indoors is not allowed, and it may be primarily due to the lack of supervision by their owner. Incompletely housetrained Pugs will not only urinate in inappropriate locations, but often have stool accidents as well. These Pugs will need constant supervision over a long period of time, combined with positive reinforcement when they eliminate in the correct location, in order to become housebroken.

PUG POINTER

In order to prevent incomplete house-training from occurring, your Pug should be given supervised access to only one or two rooms at a time. When she has successfully gone four weeks in the area without a single accident, she can be given supervised access to an additional room.

With the addition of each new room, be prepared to supervise effectively. If your Pug begins to have accidents, she isn't ready for the new area yet. Go back to confining her to the original area for an additional two to four weeks.

Incomplete housetraining should be considered as the primary cause of any Pug who regularly eliminates inappropriately; however, other issues may also be contributing to the problem.

Substrate Preferences

Substrate preferences are often exhibited by immature Pugs or puppies recently separated from their littermates or taken from their breeder. Puppies that have been raised in whelping pens or whelping boxes lined with paper may have trouble adjusting to eliminating on new surfaces. Those used to eliminating on concrete or stone surfaces may be unwilling to eliminate in grass. These puppies will seek out surfaces that are as close to the substrate as possible, often mistaking a throw rug for newspaper or a tile floor for concrete.

Pugs that eliminate inappropriately due to substrate preferences can be taught to use other surfaces in a fairly short period of time. It is a good idea to find out what surface or substrate your Pug was used to eliminating on, and then to provide that substrate in the new potty spot. You may need to get a little creative, but there are some great ways to substitute. Scraps of flooring products or imitation stone products used for patios may become a suitable substitute for concrete. Wood chips can also become a favorite substrate instead of gravel or paper.

During the housebreaking process, you will need to eliminate unsupervised access to other locations that have the same substrate, or can be confused for the preferred substrate. You will also need to verbally reward your Pug each time she eliminates in the correct spot.

Location Preferences

The most common reason that a Pug develops a location preference may actually be a combination of two factors: incomplete training and repeated punishment for having accidents. Rather than simply interrupting the dog when caught in the act and then allowing her to finish in the correct location, the Pug was severely reprimanded and often physically punished when caught having an accident. Dogs in this situation very quickly learn that it is best to sneak away to a private location instead of alerting the owner. Because positive reinforcement has not been used when the job is finished in the correct location, they often do not understand that there is another acceptable location.

Some adult Pugs develop a preference for eliminating in a specific area or room because of an aversion to their previous acceptable location. These Pugs may have initially had a frightening experience at the acceptable potty spot and begin to seek out a location that is safe and quiet. Another common location preference is near cat litter boxes. The smell of urine and stool from a feline housemate draws the Pug to that room and gives the Pug the impression that eliminating in the room is acceptable.

Marking Behaviors

Inappropriate elimination due to marking behaviors is easy to establish, but difficult to permanently correct. Marking behaviors are most commonly demonstrated by males, but female Pugs can mark as well. This behavior is most common in households where more than one dog resides. With Pugs, marking behavior is almost always limited to inappropriate urination. Marking territory is a normal dog behavior that many Pugs seem to take very seriously! While the majority of Pugs that display marking behavior are not altered, even Pugs that are neutered or spayed can exhibit inappropriate marking behaviors, particularly if they were not altered before one year of age.

Male Pugs will often mark only on vertical surfaces such as furniture, walls, curtains, or corners. The volume of urine produced at each location is generally small and in many cases more than one area is "marked." These may be near windows where the Pug can see other dogs or animals, or on or near items that have a strong odor. One common scenario is the Pug who urinates in a baby's room or on an infant's toys. The "baby smell" that is so welcomed by parents can be offensive to the Pug who has been an "only child." The decreased amount of time that the family is now spending with the Pug may cause him to re-establish his presence in the form of marking. He may begin to urinate in the room or rooms where the baby spends a great deal of time, or on items that, to his sensitive nose, have a strong scent of the baby.

Female Pugs will generally mark on horizontal surfaces, most commonly bedding. Female Pugs residing in multi-dog households may have constant conflicts over rank in the family order, and the more confident or dominant Pug will mark favorite locations with small dribbles of urine. It is also not uncommon for dominant female Pugs to urinate in the beds of children, whom they consider to be subordinate family members.

In order to decrease the frequency of marking behaviors, think supervision! It may be difficult to eliminate the scent that triggers the behavior, so it is best to eliminate access to those areas that are being targeted by your Pug. Belly bands for males or dog diapers for females may aid in keeping your possessions safe from marking. Many Pugs benefit from obedience training, combined with adopting a strategy to increase the leadership status of every family member.

Weather-Related Mistakes

Let's remember that the Pug is a toy dog. Loved, pampered, spoiled, call it what you will, this breed has a sense of entitlement. Some Pugs are quite adamant in their dislike for wet or cold weather and it is not uncommon for them to refuse to eliminate outside in bad weather, only to return to the warmth of their home and sneak off to eliminate in a private location a short time later.

Once again supervision and confinement need to be used to quickly curb this crime of opportunity and prevent it from becoming a habit. You may need to increase the number of times that your Pug is allowed outside to eliminate, since she may be determined to get back inside quickly. When a Pug is allowed to eliminate inappropriately due to weather, she is more likely to consider the household an indoor potty spot, increasing the likelihood that she will be incompletely housetrained.

You can give your Pug a better alternative during frigid temperatures or prolonged periods of bad weather. An exercise pen can be placed in the garage or in some other location that offers protection from the elements. A plastic tarp or liner can be placed under the pen, and pine shavings, potty pads, or newspapers can be placed inside the pen. By securing the plastic liner up the sides of the pen with duct tape, you create a potty area that is contained and easy to dispose of when the weather improves.

Medical Causes

Whenever a Pug eliminates inappropriately, it's a good idea to rule out any possible medical cause for the behavior. Older Pugs are particularly prone to diseases that can lead to inappropriate elimination. Diabetes mellitus, a common disease of geriatric Pugs, often causes thirst and increased urination. Cognitive dysfunction, or senility, is another medical condition of elderly Pugs. Pugs suffering from senility were once reliably housetrained, but often have a breakdown in housebreaking that gets worse over a period of time. Orthopedic diseases such as spinal disease, arthritis, or joint pain can be another cause of inappropriate elimination in middle aged to older Pugs.

Pugs are also prone to urinary tract infections and urinary stones. Pugs suffering from urinary tract problems may dribble urine in a variety of areas due to a burning sensation in the urinary tract. This inappropriate elimination may be confused with marking behavior. Adult Pugs are most commonly diagnosed with urinary tract problems, but puppies may be susceptible as well.

Pug puppies may have intestinal parasites that result in loose stools or a fast-moving digestive tract. Pug puppies may be more likely to have stool accidents if they have had recurrent diarrhea or soft stools.

A veterinarian can rule out medical causes for inappropriate elimination by completing a physical exam and performing simple tests based on the history of elimination. A visit to your veterinarian should be considered if your Pug suddenly exhibits inappropriate elimination or if, as an older Pug, she begins to have accidents over time.

PUG POINTER

Any inappropriate elimination can be frustrating to live with. A trained behaviorist can help you determine the cause(s) of the behavior and outline a treatment plan to begin training your Pug to eliminate in the appropriate location. The owner of a Pug who seeks professional help early on will be rewarded with faster, and often more permanent, results.

Rule out any possible medical causes for your Pug's inappropriate elimination behavior by contacting your veterinarian before you seek behavioral counseling.

7 *Household Manners and Obedience Basics*

Owning a well-behaved Pug doesn't happen overnight. When you first bring your Pug home, the only behaviors that he has perfected are those behaviors that are instinctual (knowing how to eliminate) and behaviors learned from interactions with littermates (biting or running away with toys). An adult Pug may have already mastered self-rewarding behaviors that allowed him to get what he wanted in his previous home (raiding trash containers, for example). He may also exhibit self-preserving moves that kept him away from trouble (such as hiding when you are angry).

Whether your Pug is a youngster or adult, teaching him household manners and basic obedience commands should be your priority. Adults can require a bit more patience especially if bad habits have already been established. You should make every effort to work with your Pug on a daily basis. Commit the time to teach a new behavior or trick, reinforce something positive, or correct a bad behavior and teach something positive in its place.

Puppy Primer

Pug puppies are easily molded. They are eager to learn, full of energy, and fun to teach. Your Pug's education should focus on learning proper social skills, perfecting good behaviors whether at home or away, and earning everything he wants from you.

The Social Butterfly

The Pug's thrive on being the center of attention. If, as puppies, they have learned how to behave in a social setting, most Pugs enjoy interactions with people and other animals. It is your responsibility to teach your Pug how to accept and properly greet strangers, as well as how to behave around other dogs.

Enrolling in a puppy socialization class or puppy kindergarten can be a fun way for your Pug to learn how to interact with other dogs. A well-run puppy class matches puppies of like temperaments and allows them to greet each other, play freely, and learn to accept corrections for overly rough play from other puppies. Puppies who are "bullies" are generally removed from play by the staff for a "time out."

Many puppy kindergarten classes also teach some basic obedience commands. A good instructor limits her class size or has enough assistants present to ensure that the playtime is properly supervised, that each owner gets the attention she needs to work with her puppy effectively, and that each puppy is happy while attending class.

Greetings!

Outside of a puppy class environment you should also look for opportunities to teach your Pug that strangers are great people to meet. Most Pugs want to greet everyone and will do anything for a treat. By combining food rewards with introductions to new people, you can quickly teach your Pug to associate meeting new people with something positive.

Take your Pug to a variety of places. Children's sports activities, the veterinary clinic, pet stores, and shopping centers are all great places to meet people. Few people can resist the cute face of a Pug, so when strangers ask if they can pet yours, tell them yes and hand them a treat. Ask each person to say "hello" to your Pug and to give him the treat upon approaching. Try to find individuals wearing hats, young children in strollers—different people in various places. Properly socialize your Pug and he will look forward to meeting everyone, regardless of their age, how they are dressed, or whether they are a man or woman.

Pugs who do not play nicely with classmates may be given a "time out."

Your Pug should be eagerly greeting people in no time, but he needs to greet them properly. Would-be greeters should only say hello to your Pug when all four of his feet are on the ground. Control the interaction by informing strangers that your Pug is learning good behavior and must not jump on them. Instruct each person to turn and quietly walk a few steps away if he jumps up. Your Pug can then approach them and try again. You can also give the *off* command accompanied by a small leash correction if he jumps up. Do not be afraid to thank your Pug's new friend for his or her time, and then simply turn and walk away from the individual if your Pug's behavior is out of control. Wait a few moments until he is no longer acting silly and out of control and then try again.

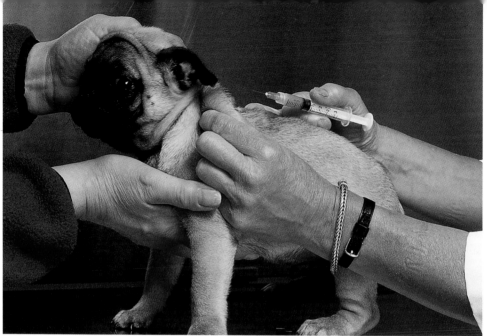
Vaccinations are necessary to protect your Pug's health.

Vaccines

Your Pug should be properly protected from potentially deadly diseases before you begin to socialize him in public. Visit your veterinarian regularly and make sure that your Pug is healthy and that he is current on all immunizations before beginning a puppy socialization class or taking him out into public. Some of the medical concerns that can result from exposure to other dogs include

- viral infections—distemper, Parvovirus, kennel cough.
- bacterial infections—leptospirosis.
- internal parasites—roundworms, hook-worms, whipworms.
- external parasites—fleas, ticks, mites.

Your veterinarian can advise you as to the right time to safely begin your Pug's public education.

Focus, Focus, Focus!

Your Pug should learn early on that you hold the keys to all things good. Teaching him to pay attention to you should be one of the first behaviors he learns. Without the ability to get your Pug's attention whenever you need it, you will have little or no control over his behavior. Try to remember that focus = control. A dog can be taught to focus on command. The first technique is to teach him to respond to his name. The second is to teach him to pay attention.

The Name Game: When you play the "name game" with your Pug you teach him to respond whenever you say his name. Look for opportunities at home to play this game—anytime your Pug is distracted by something else will do. When he is involved in an activity such as chewing on a toy simply say his name in a normal tone of voice and watch closely for a response. This may vary from turning to look at you, to stopping momentarily from chewing, or flicking an ear in your direction. The *instant* you see a response say *"good boy!"* If he continues to pay attention to you, continue to reward him verbally. A "jackpot reward" of a food treat or physical petting and rubbing can be earned by leaving his toy and coming to you.

It is important not to constantly repeat your Pug's name over and over. If you do get a response the first time, try saying the name again in a slightly higher-pitched tone of voice. Watch carefully so that you are not missing his response! Be ready to immediately reward him for any indication that you were heard.

Watch Me! Teaching your puppy to pay attention is one of the most valuable lessons you can impart. A lack of focus on the owner is usually the main reason dogs are out of control. Begin to instill this important behavior in your Pug early and he will reward you by being well behaved.

To teach this behavior, your Pug should be directly in front of you, either standing or sitting. Using your target (with a piece of food, of course), touch his nose, give the command *"watch me,"* and bring your target slowly up to your nose. Your Pug should follow the target with his head, bringing his gaze up to meet your eyes. Immediately reward him with a *"good boy"* followed by the food reward in your target. Repeat this exercise two more times. This exercise should be done several times each day. Once your Pug understands this exercise begin to slowly

increase the time he must look at you before you reward him.

If your Pug gets distracted during this exercise and looks away, simply repeat the command *"watch me"* and, if necessary, the hand signal motion from his nose to yours. Immediately reward him for returning focus to you! It is important that he get an immediate reward since he had a choice of continuing to investigate whatever distracted him. Now repeat the exercise.

Nothing in Life Is Free

"Nothing in life is free" should become your training motto. Your Pug must earn everything he wants from you, whether

Your Pug should learn to focus on you.

it is food, physical contact, play, or inter-action. This is perhaps one of the tough-est rules for Pug owners to follow. Who can resist that cute face, those big, beauti-ful eyes, and playful "woo woos"! You'll be tempted to give him anything he wants just because you are happy to have him as a part of your life. The "freebie" approach, however, teaches your Pug that he can manipulate you with his behavior. The "nothing in life is free" strategy allows you to mold his behavior into something positive.

Teaching your Pug to greet people properly is part of the "nothing in life is free" strategy. Your Pug must earn pet-ting or a food reward by remaining on the ground and not jumping. The simple behavior of "*sit*" can be used to make meals appear in his food bowl, to make doors open, or give him access to furni-ture or your lap. If your Pug must con-stantly work for the rewards in his life he will perfect good behaviors quickly.

The Role of Exercise

Fulfilling your Pug's exercise requirements is an integral part of teaching good behavior. Pugs are often thought of as fat and lazy, but young Pugs have an abun-dance of energy. Those tail-tucked out-bursts of running that he does from time to time are one way of using up excess energy. Without the opportunity to utilize this energy in a constructive way, your Pug will find some other rewarding way to get rid of it. This may include

- inappropriate chewing;
- destruction of toys, beds;

- biting or nipping;
- running, or jumping on furniture.

Excess energy also makes it difficult for your Pug to focus his attention on you or the task of learning. There is often a direct correlation between a growing, adoles-cent Pug's sudden inability to perform sim-ple behaviors that the owner believes were previously learned, and the owner's failure to commit time to exercise as part of the training routine. Adolescent Pugs need to be taken for brisk walks, enticed into a game of retrieving toys, or simply allowed to "Pug run" every day.

Prevention, Not Correction

Your training time should focus on teach-ing good behaviors right from the begin-ning of your relationship. Think in terms of prevention, not correction. If you spend your time teaching your Pug what you want him to do, he'll repeat that behavior because you have consistently rewarded it. If he learns to *sit*, and repeats this behav-ior many times each day in order to be petted, eat meals, go outside for walks, or receive a new chew bone, he'll be so busy sitting he won't have a need to investigate and learn bad behaviors.

Correct, Reward, Redirect

Eventually your Pug may learn to perform some behavior that you find objection-able. When this happens you need to be

A Pug with too much energy can be destructive and difficult to train.

able to stop the behavior and provide an alternative. You must correct him when he is misbehaving, reward him when the behavior stops, and then redirect him into a more appropriate behavior in its place.

Since Pugs love food, they are attracted to anything that smells—good or bad. Let's say your Pug has found the garbage can and is now involved in investigating its contents. You need to interrupt this behavior effectively. A shaker can—a soda can filled with coins, marbles, or rocks, and sealed with duct tape—may do the trick. Toss the shaker can at the garbage bin when your Pug is sniffing or pawing at it, interrupting this behavior. The instant that your Pug backs away you must verbally reward him! Your Pug won't know that you threw the can, so try saying "what happened?" in an upbeat tone of voice. You become the good guy and the garbage can is now bad. When your Pug comes over for comfort, a nice pat on the head is a reward for turning his attention to you. You can now redirect by teaching the leave it exercise outlined later in this chapter.

Home Schooling

Basic Obedience Commands

Sit

Sit is one of the first behaviors you should teach your Pug. It is the foundation for many other exercises, as well as the one behavior he can learn to do easily in a variety of locations. Hold your lessons in an environment that is relatively quiet and free from distractions, such as your home. Your Pug should learn to *sit* quite quickly!

To begin teaching *sit* you can use your target (a closed fist containing a treat). Begin by showing him your target. If you have not taught your Pug how to target (see in Chapter 4), you can place a food reward in between your fingers to use as a lure. Give the *sit* command and move the target or lure from his nose, raising it between his eyes and over his head between his ears. Wait for your Pug to respond by tipping his head backwards and lowering his hindquarters into the desired position. Verbally reward him immediately and give the food reward. Repeat this exercise a few more times initially, and then be ready to practice this several times each day.

If your Pug responds by jumping up toward the target or food lure, he does not yet understand what *sit* is and may be trying to touch the target instead, a behavior he already knows, or may be trying to grab for the food. This is not the behavior you want, so take the target or food lure away by pulling it up into your chest. This removes it from view, taking away any reward for jumping. Without a reward your Pug has been given a cue that jumping up is not the behavior you want. This also allows the opportunity to try some other behavior instead. Remember that this is a learning process! If he sits, be sure to reward him immediately. If he responds by backing up and away from you, try moving to a location that limits his backwards motion, in front of a wall for example. Even if he accidentally sits because he is confused, immediately give both the verbal and food reward. Remember that it is most important to initially reward for the behavior you want. You can always add the hand signal and verbal cues later if necessary.

This Pug is focused on his owner as he obeys the *sit* command.

Small food rewards should be hidden in your fist or between your fingers.

Sit is the behavior that should be most often utilized with the "nothing in life is free" strategy. Use your imagination to find ways to incorporate this behavior into your Pug's daily routine.

Down

Down is taught once your Pug knows how to *sit*. Lying down can be used to teach your Pug how to relax or can be one of the positions for the *stay* exercise later on. *Down* is one of the most challenging behaviors for most Pugs to master so be patient as he tries to learn this exercise.

To begin your Pug should be sitting in front of you. Give the command *down* and bring your target from your Pug's nose toward the floor in between his paws, and then toward you in an "L" shape. As your Pug follows the target he should move into the desired position. Make sure that he doesn't cheat! Both elbows must be on the floor in order to be rewarded.

If your Pug pops up into a standing position, take away the target and ask him to *sit* again. Don't forget to verbally

It is also permissible to help your Pug learn the correct position by using your free hand to gently guide his hindquarters toward the floor. As your target moves over the dog's head use your free hand to push him into the sitting position. Reward immediately and try again, using your free hand to help. Try simply touching your hand to his hindquarters on the third attempt instead of pushing him into the sitting position.

When your Pug is learning how to *sit* be prepared to reward him whenever you can. If you see him sitting on his own, verbally reward by saying *"good sit,"* in an effort to help him associate the sitting position with the verbal cue *"sit."* Once he has learned to associate the hand motion over his head (hand signal) and the command *sit* (verbal cue) with the desired action you can make him wait a few moments before you reward him.

Gentle pressure may help your Pug learn to lie down.

reward each *sit*. This time try moving the target from his nose to the floor in between his paws and then in toward his stomach. In order to follow the target, your Pug must drop his head, and may flop over into the *down* position by lying on his side. Be ready to immediately reward him for the correct response.

You can also place your free hand over the dog's shoulders to help guide him into the *down* position, although many Pugs will actively resist the pressure. If you are successful with this technique, begin to reduce the amount of physical help you provide. Once your Pug is lying down with little or no help from your free hand on his shoulders, try repeating the exercise using only your target hand and the command *down*.

In spite of your best efforts, your Pug may still not willingly drop into a *down* position on command. Break the exercise down into smaller parts if you have dili-

gently tried to lure him into position without success. Give him the command to *down* and lower your target toward the floor. If your Pug drops his head, reward him. Repeat the exercise over until he is lowering his head each time he hears the command. Once that is accomplished you can ask for a little more. When you give the *down* command move the target all the way to the floor and reward only if your Pug's head drops down to touch the target. Repeat this sequence. You will continue to up the ante, next rewarding him for dropping his head and moving a paw forward, then on to two paws forward, and finally for lying down. This method takes time, but for some Pugs it is the only way to successfully teach them to lie down on command.

Once your Pug has a good understanding of this exercise he may begin to go into the *down* position every time you ask him to *sit*. When this occurs he is linking the two behaviors together on his own. To change this, you must be ready to immediately reward the *sit* response before the dog has a chance to lie down. You can also begin to give the *down* command from a standing position instead of from a sitting position.

Come

Learning to come when called is one of the most important lessons your Pug can learn. Your Pug must understand that he has no other option but to come the first time you call and that each and every time he does this, there is a great reward waiting. *Come* is one of the most difficult behaviors to teach.

1. NEVER call your Pug unless he has no other choice but to *come*. That means that for a considerable length of time you will only give the command to *come* when he is on leash. You will not call him when you have no way to immediately ensure the correct response.
2. NEVER call your Pug when there is something unpleasant waiting for him. If he hates nail trims, don't say *"Pugsley, come"* with the nail trimmers visible in your hands.
3. NEVER call your Pug when you are angry or scold him when he comes to you. If you call him to come in from the yard, but he is too busy chasing birds, you have already forgotten rule number 1. If, after fifteen minutes you are now late for work because he has chosen to remain outside, and he finally reluctantly responds to your command

Your Pug should be on leash when you begin to teach him to *come* when called.

to *come*, do not scold him! Whatever happens to your Pug in the ten to fifteen seconds following his reaching you dictates whether he is likely to repeat the behavior next time.
4. ALWAYS provide a pleasurable outcome for when the *come* command is obeyed. Give a food reward every time he comes when called.
5. ALWAYS practice! Your Pug will only learn to *come* when called if you commit a significant amount of time teaching him that this behavior is both mandatory and rewarding.

Begin teaching him this behavior as soon as possible. If your Pug is never given the opportunity to learn that he has the option to either disobey or escape, his response to the command *come* will be reliable. Likewise, if he believes that coming when called produces good results, his response will be reliable. You must be willing to spend as much time as necessary to teach this behavior.

Teaching the exercise indoors in a small area will limit your Pug's ability to escape or ignore your commands. To begin, walk up to your Pug, call his name, followed by *come*, in a happy, upbeat tone of voice and show him your target. If he has been target trained he already knows that moving forward to touch the target produces a reward. He should eagerly move forward a few inches to touch the target. Immediately reward him. This step should be repeated at least ten to fifteen times each day for at least two weeks. Once your Pug begins to associate the word sequence with moving toward the target you can begin to back away from him for a short

Immediately reward your Pug every time he comes to you.

If your Pug fails to move in your direction, give a slight leash correction by popping toward you on the leash, moving backwards away from the dog, and verbally encouraging him to move toward you. You may have to pull him toward you the majority of the way, almost like reeling in a fish. Regardless of whether he comes to you voluntarily or is pulled in, you must continue reward food and verbal praise. Your Pug must learn that compliance with this command is mandatory. He will respond much better when rewarded. Repeat the exercise two more times. By practicing this exercise three to four times each day for a week your Pug will learn to "*come*" when called and be rewarded consistently. The next week try rewarding verbally every time, but only provide a food reward every second time. The third week, your Pug gets verbally rewarded every time, and food rewarded every third time.

distance. This step should also be repeated at least ten to fifteen times each day for two weeks. Once his response is reliable at a short distance you can begin to work on adding a little distance.

Distance work is done in several ways. The first is to attach a leash or long line to the dog's collar. Holding on to one end let your Pug get distracted at a distance. Give the *come* command and show him your target (which can be held either along your leg or in front of your knees). If he moves in your direction, praise him continuously in an excited tone of voice. Allow him to have the food reward when he reaches you. The more excitement you display for even the slightest movement forward, the more quickly your Pug will continue to move toward you.

Distance can be slowly increased by using a long line. When you have an immediate response to the command without having to give a physical pop correction, try giving him five or ten more feet. If you have to give a correction to get him started in your direction, go back to a shorter distance. Reward your Pug for every movement in your direction, no matter how small. Eventually you should be able to drop the line altogether and call him to you. If he fails to *come* when called, step on the leash to stop any forward movement and administer a pop in your direction. Remember to go slowly— it may take many months of daily practice to ensure reliable behavior.

The second way to teach *come* from a distance is to play "ping pong." This game should be played in a secure area and requires two or more players. Each person should have a supply of yummy food rewards. Begin by standing ten to fifteen feet apart. One person issues the *come* command, shows the target and encourages the dog to move toward it. Once he reaches the target, he is verbally rewarded and receives the food reward. Another player repeats the same sequence followed by another player. Your Pug learns to respond quickly to the command, bouncing back and forth between players like a ping-pong ball. Play the game daily for at least two weeks. During the second week, the first person rewards with food, but the second person only provides verbal praise. When playing with three or more people, every other correct response produces a food reward. Remember that every response should produce a verbal reward!

The third way is to play the "struggling catch me" game. You will need someone to help you with this exercise. Begin in an area that limits your Pug's ability to leave, such as a hallway. Your helper holds the dog by the collar, without talking to him, while you walk away from him. When you are at a distance, turn and say your Pug's name in an excited tone of voice. Remember that Pugs like interaction, so your goal here is to get him so excited that he tries to break away from the person holding him. When he is focused on you and struggling to get to you, give him the *come* command and encourage him to make a beeline straight to you. Reward immediately for coming to you.

Stay

Stay is a command that needs to be built up slowly over time. Your goal is for your Pug to begin to understand that you expect him to remain in one place until you give a release word such as "*free*" or "*break.*" To do this you must begin in an area with very few distractions and expect him to stay for a very short time—only a few seconds. Each time you ask your Pug to *stay*, you should perform the exercise three to four times in a row. Each day, you should be able to increase the length of time for the *stay*, working up to a minute or more.

Place your Pug on a leash to begin this exercise. The lead should be held in your right hand. Ask him to *sit* in heel position on your left side and verbally reward the response. Give the *stay* command and use the flat palm of your left hand extended in front of you (toward the nose) as the signal to remain in the sitting position. Your voice command should be deep and authoritative in tone. With your right leg moving first, step directly in front of your Pug, pause in front for a second, step back into *heel* position, and wait a second or two *before* you giving the release command "*free.*" The release word should be in a high-pitched, happy tone of voice to let him know that the exercise is over. If he moves before you return, a jerk up on the leash, accompanied by a stern "*egh*" or "*no*" should stop him from moving any further. Ask your Pug to *sit* and *stay* and try again.

If your Pug gets up from the sitting position before you release him you have missed the opportunity to correct him.

Your outstretched arm, with a flat palm toward your Pug, is the signal to *stay*.

Day 1—Sit/stay for five seconds, standing directly in front.

Day 2—Sit/stay for eight seconds, standing directly in front.

Day 3—Sit/stay for fifteen seconds, standing directly in front.

Day 4—Sit/stay for twenty seconds, standing directly in front.

Day 5—Sit/stay for thirty seconds, standing directly in front.

Day 6—Sit/stay for five seconds, two steps in front.

Day 7—Sit/stay for eight seconds, two steps in front.

Day 8—Sit/stay for fifteen seconds, two steps in front.

Day 9—Sit/stay for twenty seconds, two steps in front.

Day 10—Sit/stay for thirty seconds, two steps in front.

Increase the time and distance over alternate weeks.

Ask him to *sit* again and repeat the exercise, diligently watching for any signs of movement (head tilting downward, sniffing, focus on something behind you or to the side). Use your leash and your voice to correct him the instant he begins to move out of position, not when he is already standing or lying down.

Don't ask your Pug to stay too long or move away too quickly. Remember, this exercise is about building up to a longer time and a longer distance. You can increase only the time or distance each time; not both at the same time. If you are training this exercise each day, try increasing the time by fifteen-second intervals one week and then increase the distance by a foot or two the next week. A typical training schedule might look like this:

Hints

■ A tired Pug is likely to perform a better *down* and *stay*, than a *sit* and *stay*! He may prefer to lie down than to sit.

■ The time that your Pug is capable of staying in one place is largely dependent on his age. Puppies have shorter attention spans. A well-executed *stay* exercise for a puppy may be only ten to fifteen seconds in length. Adult Pugs can quickly learn to *stay* for up to a minute.

■ Teaching *stay* in a hallway or on stairs will limit your Pug's ability to move out of position.

Your Pug can be taught to stay in a *down* position too.

■ If your Pug cannot succeed at a higher distance or increased time, go back one step so that he can successfully complete the exercise. Repeat this step for an additional day or two, rewarding each successful *stay*, and then try again to increase the time or distance.

Wait

Wait is a command that tells your Pug to freeze in position and, upon your release word, continue to move forward. *Wait* is also the command that typically proceeds *come* in obedience competitions. *Wait* can be used with any position; sitting, standing, or lying down. Your Pug should learn to *wait* while you wipe his muddy paws and before proceeding through any door.

The easiest way to teach this command is to use a doorway. First, make sure that your Pug is on leash and walk toward the door. Give the *sit* and verbally reward the response. Give the *wait* command and use the open, flat palm of your hand in a small waving motion or one finger (as if you are saying, *"Just one moment"*) to indicate the command. Begin to open the door and when your Pug moves, give a small jerk backwards on the leash and a sharp *"no"* or *"egh"* as you also close the door. Repeat the *sit* and w*ait* commands. It will take a few attempts, but each time he'll get better and soon you'll have the door open while your Pug sits patiently. Give the release word *"free"* and allow him to walk outside. The more you practice, the sooner you'll be able to have him *wait* with the door wide open!

You can also teach *wait* when your Pug is walking in *heel* position. Stop moving and give the *wait* command. If your Pug continues walking forward, give a little tug backwards and repeat the command. Wait for him to stop in place either sitting or standing. Once he remains motionless for a few seconds, give him the release word and proceed to moving forward.

Training Options

Teaching your Pug to be obedient happens primarily at home, through a lot of dedicated time and effort on your part. It may seem like a daunting task at times, and you may find it necessary to employ the help of others to successfully get the job done. Finding someone to help you train your Pug can be a big step in sealing that bond you have together. But the wrong trainer or training situation can also create additional problems for both you and your Pug. How do you know who is the right person for the job? Learning the pros and cons of different training options will help you make the right decision.

Obedience Classes

An obedience class can be a fun, inexpensive way to expose your Pug to more distractions, and the instructors can be valuable in helping you mold his behavior. Obedience classes may be offered through your local park district, sponsored by a local kennel club, or offered at a boarding kennel or day care center. Classes generally meet once a week for one hour. They can vary in length from six to eight weeks.

Your veterinarian may be able to give you a recommendation on which classes are best. Don't be afraid to inquire about the class before you sign up. If there is more than one class offered you will need to ask which class is best suited to you and your Pug. Find out what the student to instructor ratio is for any class. Too many students and not enough teachers can be a recipe for disaster!

Personal Trainers

A personal trainer will work with you and your Pug in your home. This can be very beneficial if you cannot locate a class that is convenient for you. Some personal trainers only teach basic obedience while others offer behavioral counseling to help

---

PUG POINTER

Obedience trainers are not universally regulated or certified. Anyone can claim to be a trainer, so you must do your research.

Ask these questions:

- *Are you a certified dog trainer? If yes, which certification program? May I have a copy of your certificate? Many good trainers are not certified.*
- *How long have you been a professional dog trainer?*
- *What method(s) do you use to teach?* **Remember that Pugs often learn best when initially taught using reward-based or positive reinforcement training.**
- *May I have a list of references? May I visit your class?*
- *Do you belong to any professional training organizations? (The Association of Pet Dog Trainers and the International Association of Canine Professionals are two leading dog organizations for professional dog trainers.)*
- *Do you have references from any local veterinarians?*

---

change problem behaviors. Personal trainers are often more expensive than obedience classes and the best ones may be unavailable to provide lessons on a regular basis because of their busy schedules. A good personal trainer will find out what your goals are before outlining a training plan. They will not only demonstrate techniques first and help your Pug learn new behaviors, but will also teach you how to work with him between sessions.

Board and Train

Some kennels and trainers offer a service that allows you to leave the dog at their facility for a specific period of time to learn basic commands. Board and train options should be considered carefully as they can have some significant drawbacks. First, you must find out exactly where your Pug will be housed during his stay and exactly how much time each day will be spent focused on training. Second, inquire as to the method and type of equipment that will be used during training. Many trainers offering this option do not train using reward-based techniques and may use prong collars for quick results. The majority of Pugs will not respond to forced training and may become withdrawn or nervous. Finally, ask how you will learn to work with your Pug when he goes home. Board and train is an expensive training option and in order for it to continue to work at home you must learn the same signals and be consistent in working with your Pug every day once he is home.

Many Pugs do not enjoy boarding away from home. If yours is too stressed by the environment, he will be unable to concentrate on learning. This may be viewed as stubbornness by some trainers. If the stress of boarding is combined with force training, your Pug will only suffer anxiety and may come home confused and fearful. In addition, some behaviors such as housebreaking your Pug cannot be addressed by leaving him with someone else to be trained.

Daily training is a great way to bond with your Pug.

Home Schooling

Manners

Some behaviors are specifically needed at home. As such you won't find these commands in an obedience ring, but they are equally as important as basic obedience.

Drop It!

This command should become a learned response for the dog to immediately open his mouth and spit out whatever is in it. Consider this behavior a necessity, as it may save your Pug's life one day! Most Pug puppies pick up household objects to see what they do, but if you come screaming at them, attempting to pry the object from their mouth, they do what they would do if a littermate was trying to take something away from them—RUN! It becomes a game of "I stole it; therefore you will chase me!"

Teaching Your Pug to Drop Objects on Command

1. *Drop it* needs to be set up at least once every day for a minimum of two weeks in a situation that you control (not a stolen item scenario). This behavior must become routine and the only way to teach it is to set your Pug up every day to succeed over an extended period of time. You will need to find a food reward that he considers of high value and have it with you. Find an item of medium interest to your Pug—a crumpled-up paper towel—for example, and use it to teach *drop it*. Your Pug should be on leash (so that he cannot run away). Toss the paper towel onto the floor in front of your Pug. Allow him to pick it up and in a stern voice give the *drop it* command as you put the food reward right in front of his nose (think of this as a trade for the paper towel). Your Pug now has a choice to make. As soon as he drops the item, verbally reward him and give him the food reward. Do this several times in a row until he is no longer picking up the object. The next time, try a different "set up" object if he won't take the paper towel right from the start.

   If your Pug is chewing on a favorite bone, walk up to him calmly with the food reward and give the *drop it* command. When he gives up the bone in exchange for the treat, verbally reward him. He can then *sit* to have his bone returned to him. This also teaches your Pug to relinquish items to you and minimizes resource guarding in the future (a behavior all dogs learn to some degree). Some Pugs may learn to inappropriately carry this behavior over to you at the food dish or over rawhide bones or other items of high value. If your Pug becomes aggressive around any toys or food, seek the help of a professional behavioral counselor.

2. If your Pug has something he shouldn't and it isn't dangerous DO NOT CHASE HIM! Find something that will catch his attention (squeezing a potato chip bag works wonders, for example!) and when

he is no longer running, praise him! Walk calmly up to him with the potato chip bag and say *"Drop it"* as you offer him a chip in exchange for the item. You don't have to go looking for "dog food"; any item you have that can be considered higher value than the stolen item will work. Use your imagination! Pieces of apple, popcorn, and sandwich meats may all work as a high value reward. Take whatever is handy at that moment.

3. If your Pug begins to run away, or goes into a play bow, turn your back on him. He may try to figure out why you won't engage in play and often will drop the item and come to you to see what's up. Don't forget to praise him!

4. Remember that while you are teaching *drop it* the item you offer in trade must be higher in value than the item he has. It is important to know the canine currency value of food rewards or items that your Pug enjoys.

5. The more you set your Pug up to successfully relinquish items, the faster he'll learn this behavior. The longer you reward him for doing so, the more consistently he'll *drop it* when he has stolen an item. Eventually no longer having a food reward to reclaim those stolen items meets the criteria for intermittent reward.

Leave It

This is the "sister" command to *drop it*. All dogs should learn to leave things alone upon the owner's command. Once again it can be a life-saving command! Dogs lead with their noses, and that means that your

Pug will be interested in anything that smells. Once something is interesting he'll investigate it by attempting to pick it up.

Once the *leave it* command is learned you can use it around the house and on walks to keep your Pug walking right by interesting things on the ground, people, and even other dogs. You may prefer to use *"Ick"* or *"Not yours"* instead of *"leave it."* Whichever command you choose, make sure everyone is consistently using the same words.

Teaching *Leave It*

1. Set up your Pug for *leave it* at least once a day for a minimum of two weeks. You'll find lots of times where this command comes in handy! It should always be done on leash at first. Pick an object that your puppy may find particularly interesting. Toss it on the floor in front of him, close enough that he believes he has a chance to get it, but far enough away that you can stop him with the leash. As soon as he moves toward the object, give a sharp tug on the leash and give the *leave it* command in a firm tone of voice. You may need to repeat the command each time your Pug moves toward the object again. When he finally halts his attempts to move toward the object, verbally reward him with a *"good boy."* If he turns to come back to you, encourage him to do so, and when he makes it all the way to you give a bonus food reward and physical petting.

Repeat these steps. You'll find that each time that your Pug has a choice to make, he'll think about it. When he

A Pug's favorite place to "settle" is usually on the couch.

makes a conscious decision to leave the object alone (looks at it and then looks at you without moving toward the object), verbally reward him and end the training session.

Your Pug will soon learn that when the leash is on, it is a set-up and he won't attempt to touch items that you put in front of him. You can either try to use something that is more appealing, such as food placed on a chair or on the floor, or try using the original object without the leash. If you do not have the leash, be ready to stomp on the floor as you say "*leave it*" in order to interrupt his behavior.

2. If your Pug gets hold of the object, either because you were too close to it or he is off leash, it is now time to use your *drop it* command.

3. The more you set him up to successfully leave items alone, the faster your Pug will learn this behavior. Once he's mastered it, continue to reward him each time he does it correctly. You can then begin to give a food reward every other time he successfully leaves something alone. After another week or two you can try rewarding every third or fourth time.

4. Every time your Pug voluntarily moves away from an object when you say "*leave it*" you must remember to acknowledge the accomplishment with verbal praise.

To Your Spot

Teaching your Pug to go to a particular location when told can be a great idea. Your Pug can be taught to go to a rug or bed on command and that command can be used whenever the doorbell rings, when you sit down to eat a meal, or any time you want some quiet time alone.

The goal is for the dog to immediately move to a designated location on command, and to sit or lie quietly until you release him. That sequence involves too many different behaviors to teach at one time. You must teach the individual parts and then string them together.

First, your Pug must associate the specific location with something good. Using a small rug or bed allows you to take his "spot" wherever you go! Start the exercise on-leash and keep a good supply of treats. Give the *settle* or *on your mat* command and use your target to guide him to the rug. You can also toss a treat onto the rug. As soon as he has one foot on the rug reward by giving an additional treat! Move back a few feet and repeat the exercise two to four more times.

The next day ask your Pug to *settle* and reward for one foot on the rug on the first attempt. Your Pug should have two feet on the rug in order to receive the food reward on each of the following three attempts. You may need to lead him farther onto the rug at first so that both feet are on the rug.

On the third day give the *settle* command and reward him for two feet on the rug for the first time and then all four feet on the rug for the next three or four times. For the next week your Pug should make a beeline for his rug each time you practice the *settle* command and get a ver-

bal reward followed by a food reward from your target.

Next we want to teach your Pug to go to the rug and *sit* automatically. Your Pug should still be on leash for this exercise. Give the *settle* command and wait for her to walk onto the rug. Verbally reward him for going to the spot and give the *sit* command. You might need to use your hand signal as an additional cue for sitting on the rug. As soon as his hindquarters are on the rug, immediately reward him both verbally and with the food. Repeat this exercise two more times and quit for the day. For the next ten days you will ask your Pug to *settle* and reward him for going to the rug and sitting.

When your Pug is sitting automatically it is time to add the *stay* exercise. Ask your Pug to *settle* and wait for his response. If you are doing your homework he should go to the rug and immediately *sit*. Verbally reward him and give the *stay* command. Count to five, give him the release word, and reward him. You can now build up the length of time he must remain on the rug before being released.

If you try to work this exercise in a different location you may need to go back to rewarding some of the original steps. Remember that Pugs learn by doing the same things over and over, and location can be a big factor in whether yours is consistent on an exercise. Distractions are different in each place so be prepared to reward him often by breaking the exercise down into the individual parts before putting them all together.

Teaching Tricks

Pugs are natural clowns so teaching your Pug to perform tricks can be easy. Many Pugs love to "talk," some love to give their paws, others enjoy playing dead or rolling over. The key to teaching any trick is to first know what you want your Pug to do. Next you must reward behaviors that are close to, or a component of, the exercise. You must then link these individual pieces together, rewarding each component as it occurs. After much practice, you will have your Pug performing tricks and must reward the final result. What your Pug can learn to do is only limited by your imagination.

Shake

Teaching your Pug to shake hands is usually easy because they love to use their front feet. Begin by asking your Pug to *sit*. Give your Pug the command to *shake*, touch his leg, and lift it off of the floor. Immediately reward the lift even if you had to pick the leg up. Repeat this exercise several more times.

On day two repeat the exercise, lifting the leg if necessary. On the second attempt, give the *shake* command and touch, but do not pick up, the leg. Wait to see if your Pug moves it forward all on his own. Reward him for doing so. Repeat this several times.

Each subsequent day you should help your Pug a little less. Pretty soon you will be giving the *shake* command, and as you reach forward his paw will meet your hand. This is the point for a bonus

reward—get really excited and let him know that you are pleased. Most dogs favor one paw over the other—think of it as being right-pawed or left-pawed. If your Pug seems to have trouble grasping the concept of *shake*, try working with the opposite paw.

Play Dead

Your Pug must voluntarily lie down in order to learn this exercise. Give the *down* command. Introduce the command *bang* and, using a food lure move the food sideways from his head toward the floor. At the same time take your other hand and gently push your Pug into a roll and onto the hip that is on the same side as your directional hand movement. Begin by rewarding any slight movement in the correct direction no matter how small. You will eventually want him to roll onto his side when he hears the command *bang*. This trick can take time to teach. Your Pug must trust you enough to allow you to push him onto his side. Do not try to force him into that position. He will learn much quicker if you reward little movements in the right direction. If he becomes scared or worried, he won't want to perform the trick and may begin to refuse to *down* on command.

At first you will food reward small movements toward lying on his side. Then for a period of time, you will begin to only give the food reward for a full flop. Next you will want to give the food reward only when your Pug is on his side and with his head on the floor too!

When your Pug is comfortably rolling onto his side with his head down it is time

Pugs are natural clowns. They love to learn tricks.

to add the "*wait*" command. Teaching him to lie on his side and wait until he is released means he must understand the concept of waiting for a signal to move again. Give him the command *bang* and when he flops onto his side give the command *wait*. Count silently to three and then release him and give him the food reward.

Roll Over

This is actually an extension of the behavior of playing dead. Give the *bang* command and wait for the response. Next give the command *roll over* and physically roll your Pug over using his legs. Reward him! Repeat this exercise two more times. Eventually you may find that he attempts to roll over all on his own. Reward him for any attempt to roll over even if it fails. Pugs don't have a streamlined body shape and moving that much mass takes some effort!

Try helping your Pug to flip over if he attempts the roll on his own. Once again this behavior takes time for many Pugs to learn, so patience and properly timed rewards are the keys.

8 *Dealing with Bad Behaviors*

Pugs with bad manners are difficult to live with. Rescue organizations are constantly rehabilitating Pugs that were given up because the owner could no longer tolerate bad behavior. In many instances the behavior likely could have been minimized or even prevented with some early training.

This chapter will explore some of the most common behavioral problems that Pugs develop, the reasons behind the behavior, and how to properly manage them. It is important to remember that in order to change some behaviors you may need to seek the help of a professional dog trainer or behavioral therapist.

Exercise and Bad Behaviors

Quite often, Pugs need exercise and activities to keep them occupied and busy. This energy requirement varies from one Pug to the next and can be related to age. This means that your Pug may need more than just a short walk two or three times a day, especially if she is under a year old.

A young Pug unstimulated by mental and physical exercise often exhibits destructive behavior. A bored Pug may begin to bark, jump up, or dig at your legs in an effort to gain your attention. When your Pug cannot release excess energy by running around, tail tucked and full speed ahead, she will find some other creative way to blow off steam. You may not find her creativity quite as amusing as she does!

There are ways to help your Pug meet her energy requirements:

- Brisk, fast-paced walks (not potty trips) at least three times per day.
- Training sequences of quick, repetitive behaviors such as *sit* and *down.*
- Toys that can be filled or stuffed with treats, making them interactive and rewarding.
- Doggie day care or puppy "play dates" with other canine friends.

Extinguishing Bad Behaviors

In order to change your Pug's bad behavior(s) you must know what is reinforcing them. In other words, what reward is your Pug receiving each time she does the specific behavior? Is she receiving a physical reward by touching you? Is she obtaining a food reward or verbal reinforcement?

Remember that a food reward from a Pug's perspective is anything edible. That does not necessarily mean that the reward is food. To some Pugs paper, plastic, or other items may be considered quite a treat.

Extinction of a behavior occurs when a conditioned response is reduced or eliminated by taking away what reinforces it. Simply put, if your Pug is no longer rewarded for a bad behavior, over time that behavior will go away. If you can reduce or eliminate the perceived reward, over time you reduce the chance that the behavior will be repeated.

Understanding this concept is important if you want to change a bad behavior. For many bad behaviors there are no quick fixes or shortcuts. You need to be willing to work for as long as it takes in order to change bad behavior to good behavior.

Puppy Mouthing and Biting

Biting, mouthing, and nipping are all very normal behaviors for a Pug puppy. The only way your Pug knows how to play is to interact with you as she would with her littermates. Normal puppy play involves chasing, tackling, and biting, which may be also accompanied by growling or barking. This behavior is most often directed at toddlers, small children, or adults who are lying or sitting on the floor. Baggy clothing, socks (along with the toes beneath them), and shoelaces are also favorite targets of play biting. If it moves and it is within reach of young puppy's teeth, it is fair game!

Fortunately, normal play biting is an age-related behavior. Pugs typically exhibit this behavior between the ages of eight weeks and four months of age. By five to six months of age, the behavior normally decreases in frequency and intensity.

While biting behavior is normal, it doesn't change the fact that it really hurts! In order to survive the assault of needle teeth you need to take a two-step approach. You must teach that biting is not a behavior that will be tolerated, and provide her another alternative that can effectively satisfy the need to play.

Bite Inhibition

If your Pug had littermates she already knows about "bite inhibition." Bite inhibition is knowing how hard to bite without causing pain or damage to her playmate. If play among puppies becomes too rough and biting becomes too hard, the puppy that is being bitten will yelp sharply in pain. This a verbal cue that tells the biter to let go and that she is biting too hard. If you can replicate or mimic this cue by sharply saying "*Ow,*" your puppy should immediately let go of whatever she is biting. Any sound that you can use to interrupt biting behavior is acceptable. You should then immediately redirect to a play activity that is appropriate. Try giving her a tug toy or chew bone and praise her for playing appropriately with the new object.

Young children may be unable to make a sound that is strong enough to interrupt biting behavior. Interactions between dogs and children should always be properly supervised, and if you cannot effectively stop your puppy from nipping his human

A tired Pug is a well-behaved Pug.

siblings, it is best to separate them and give your Pug something else to play with.

Factors Affecting Biting Behaviors

Puppy biting can be directly related to

- **Movement.** Walking or running draws attention to you. Clothing that moves or flows becomes an interactive toy. Children have body movements that are often exaggerated, making them instant targets for play biting.
- **Location.** Anyone or anything that is within reach is in the "play zone." That means that feet and legs, particularly those of children, are all potential play targets. If you are holding your Pug on your lap, your fingers, arms, and face are all easily within reach and may become biting targets.
- **Energy.** Puppies with too much energy often have a harder time inhibiting their biting behavior. If your Pug lacks exercise she is likely to escalate her biting behavior during periods of play.
- **Body Language.** Seemingly harmless interactions, such as making eye contact, can escalate biting behavior during play.
- **Voice.** High-pitched sounds signal play behavior. Pugs are drawn to the high-pitched voices of children and her efforts to play with them often turn quickly to biting. A bite then brings screeches and tears that are often misinterpreted as additional play signals.

Managing Puppy Biting and Mouthing

Biting behavior in a puppy is normal. To minimize how many opportunities your Pug has to nip at her human family, you must learn to manage her during her peak periods of activity. It is unrealistic to expect a puppy to never nip, mouth, or play bite. You can, however, teach her to use bite inhibition, to play softly, and to stop play biting on command.

1. The rule of thumb should be no out of control nipping or biting. This means your Pug should never bite hard enough to leave a mark or draw blood. For homes with small children a better rule of thumb is *"no teeth should ever contact skin."*
2. If your Pug applies only gentle pressure during play, quietly praise her.
3. If she bites too hard, immediately yell *"Ouch!"* or *"Ow!,"* loud enough to startle your puppy and make her back away. Praise her in a soothing tone of voice if she does. Redirect her play behavior to an acceptable toy.
4. If your Pug is overly stimulated and cannot exhibit self-control (bite inhibition) confine her to an area such as a crate or exercise pen. When she is calm, you can allow her to be with you again.
5. Biting behaviors typically occur around periods of activity in a household. Be prepared to provide interactive toys during these periods to preempt play biting.
6. Training sequences can also be used to preempt play biting.

To teach your Pug how to stop play biting on command you will need to practice the following routine on a daily basis:

1. Choose a word that will give your Pug permission to take food from your hand. *Okay* or *yes* can be successfully used for this exercise.
2. To get your Pug's attention, place a treat in front of her. Say the word *"yes"* and give the treat.
3. Offer another treat and as she moves to take it from you, say *"Ow!"* in a firm tone of voice, but do not yell. If your Pug backs away and does not attempt to take the food from you for two or three seconds, give the *yes* command and give her the treat. If she touches your hand in an attempt to get the treat before two or three seconds have passed, yell *"Ow!"* immediately. Your goal is to make the dog back away, so say it like you mean it!
4. Repeat these steps, slowly increasing the time your Pug must wait before receiving her food reward.
5. When she has learned to back away on command, you may then begin to practice without food in your hand. Try to find situations that are slightly more stimulating and practice this routine during those periods of excitement.

Destructive Chewing

Chewing is a natural behavior for dogs. Pugs chew to relieve boredom or stress, to relieve the discomfort from teething, or as a way to release energy. Some Pugs chew just because it feels good. Others

PUG POINTER

You can make your own interactive toy by placing a handful of food into a plastic water or soda bottle that has been rinsed out, dried, and has had the label removed.

Place the bottle on the floor. Your Pug must now figure out how to get the food out of the bottle. As the bottle is knocked over or rolled around on the floor, it makes an interesting noise, much like a baby rattle.

If she tips it over just right, your Pug will be rewarded by spilling food out onto the floor. As she grabs the bottle, the plastic will collapse creating another interesting sound.

If the plastic begins to crack, replace the bottle with a new one to avoid sharp edges.

This toy should be used under supervision for those occasions when you find it necessary to keep your Pug occupied within the area you are working.

If she is an adult, your Pug is more likely to chew destructively when she is left alone. Destructive chewing can be a sign of separation anxiety, a behavioral problem common in Pugs adopted from shelters or rescue groups. No one really knows why some Pugs exhibit separation anxiety while others do not; however, this condition often requires both medication and behavioral modification in order to help overcome the anxiety.

Managing Destructive Chewing

Destructive chewing can be controlled. First, make sure your Pug is always supervised—especially if she is a puppy. A properly supervised puppy is more likely to be engaged in activities that involve interactions with family members. Interactive play leaves little time to find something else to hold her attention, such as a chair leg or the corner of a wall.

Second, whenever your Pug cannot be supervised she should be confined to her crate or placed in an acceptable play area. A puppy playpen keeps your Pug safe from chewing on potentially dangerous objects such as electrical cords. If you choose to confine him to a small room, remember that those teeth and front feet can be used to put holes in drywall very quickly!

Finally, your Pug must be given activities that she finds rewarding. Choose toys that are amusing and attractive to her, providing her with stimulating and interactive fun. Look for the following in your choice of playthings for your Pug:

chew to explore their environment. If your Pug chews on items that are inappropriate, it is important to try to discover the underlying reason for her behavior. Is she bored during the day when he is alone? Is she stressed or anxious?

The only way to stop inappropriate chewing is to better manage her environment, thereby eliminating the ability to be destructive. You cannot train your Pug not to chew, but you can prevent her from doing so. This behavior is one of opportunity. Puppies are most likely to exhibit this behavior during adolescence (from twelve weeks of age to six months of age).

Your Pug should learn to take treats nicely.

■ Makes interesting noises or sounds.
■ Sustains movement.
■ Rewards play by spilling food or treats or "feeds" by coming apart into pieces.

Your Pug doesn't need every toy in the pet store. What she does need is a few toys that she cannot wait to play with. Rawhide bones, dried meat products, and vegetable-based chew bones will all hold your Pug's interest for some time. She should be given toys that she can safely chew and destroy, without causing harm to herself. Rawhide toys should not be small enough to be swallowed. Any small pieces should be thrown away. Your Pug should always be supervised while chewing on rawhide bones.

Managing Separation Anxiety

If your Pug suffers from separation anxiety there are no simple, quick ways to change her behavior. Separation anxiety is often best managed by improving the environment in which she is left alone, instituting behavioral changes, and using appropriate medications as prescribed by your veterinarian. If you think your Pug may suffer from this condition, you should first contact your veterinarian or a behavioral therapist for help in diagnosing this disorder. You can also begin to make changes to your routine both at home and when you prepare to leave.

■ Do not reinforce or reward attention-seeking behaviors. If your Pug is a

"Velcro" dog, following you everywhere, quietly praise her whenever she is not in physical contact with you.
■ Teach your Pug to *settle* and *stay* on command. Begin this training at a close distance, gradually increasing the distance as you move farther away.
■ Desensitize your Pug to your departure cues. Make a list of the things you do before you leave. Now do these things out of order and at random times each day. Pick up your keys or coat and carry them around while you do housework, ignoring any response from your Pug.
■ Turn on the radio or television at least thirty minutes before you depart. This provides background noise.

- Avoid giving attention before you leave. Ignore your Pug for fifteen to thirty minutes before you depart.
- Don't confine your Pug to a crate if she has not been crate trained; it may increase anxiety. Confinement can be used if she is already comfortable within a specific area.
- Consider doggie day care as an alternative to leaving your Pug alone.
- Make sure that your departure is low key.
- Provide stimulating toys to play with during your absence.
- Do not make a big fuss when you return.

- Once your Pug has settled down and is calm, reward with low-key physical contact.
- Do not scold or punish for accidents or destructiveness during your absence. This generally increases anxiety and may make your Pug avoid you upon your return.

Caught in the Act

If you should catch your Pug chewing on something inappropriate, interrupt her behavior by making a sharp noise. A shake can, thrown in the direction of the object she is chewing, or a book, dropped on the floor, are both effective interruptions. If done correctly, your Pug may believe that the object actually produced the sound, which can create an aversion to further chewing at that location. As soon as she stops chewing, provide her with a suitable chew toy and praise her for chewing on that instead. Bitter-type sprays, applied to areas that your Pug finds attractive, may also help create an aversion to chewing.

Begging for Food

Do you consider it begging for food if your Pug is staring at you while you eat? Or is she begging only if she makes physical contact with you by jumping up on your legs? Each person's definition of begging is different so you must have a clear idea of what it is you want your Pug to do whenever food is present.

The best strategy is to not allow your Pug to learn bad table manners at all.

Some Pugs are anxious about being left alone.

Whenever you are eating, confine her in an area away from the table. If she is consistently kept away from the dining area, she cannot jump on you for attention, and she will not inadvertently be rewarded by food accidentally or intentionally dropped on the floor. More importantly, she learns that the table area is off limits to her at mealtime. She can be fed in her crate at the same time you eat, or be given a special treat to keep her busy. If you do decide to give her a meal in her crate at the same time you have your meals, make sure that you can get her outside before she has an accident in her crate.

If your Pug has already learned that the dining room table is a buffet for her you will need to adopt a new plan. You can crate her or confine her to another room, but you will need to make sure that she has something to keep her busy. This is another great time for an interactive toy. If your Pug begins to bark, ignore her until she is quiet. If you go to her, either to scold her or let her out, you will be inadvertently rewarding the barking behavior.

If you choose not to confine your Pug, you will need to ignore her completely at meal time. If she jumps on you with her front paws, simply ignore her. Do not look at her or attempt to push her away, as this only reinforces the behavior by rewarding her with physical contact. It may take several meals but eventually your Pug will learn that jumping on you brings no response. This is a great time to teach her to sit quietly or lie down at mealtime.

To begin teaching your Pug to sit while you eat you will need to have something readily available to reward her for the correct behavior. Instead of feeding her a bowl of food for dinner, use her meal as training treats. It is also a good idea to keep her on leash so that she cannot go visiting others at the table. When you sit down to eat ask your Pug to *sit*. If she complies, verbally reward her and quietly give the treat. You should begin eating. If she continues to sit patiently, reward her again. If she jumps on you, ignore her until she has all four feet on the floor. Immediately ask her to *sit* and reward her again for complying. Repeat this exercise throughout dinner. Each meal thereafter, your Pug should be rewarded for sitting and ignored for any other behavior. Over time, she will learn to sit quietly while you enjoy your meal.

Roaming or Running Away

Some Pugs are homebodies, preferring to hang around the house rather than visit the neighbors. Other Pugs, particularly those in adolescence, are quite curious about the world they live in. These Pugs will wander off in search of a new friend or find themselves lost after chasing away birds or squirrels.

It can be a terrifying experience if your Pug wanders off. It's also a dangerous and potentially fatal habit for her to learn. The reason for your Pug's wanderlust can be related to boredom, hormonal influences, or simply because she has successfully passed through the doorway many times before.

Your Pug should never be left outside alone, especially if your yard is not securely fenced. Isolation leads to boredom. A bored Pug looks for any opportunity she can to interact with people or other animals.

Your Pug is also much more likely to wander if he is not altered. Male Pugs that are intact may have only one thing on their mind, and when enticed by the scent of a female in season, they'll travel great distances in search of that girlfriend. Female Pugs have also been known to take trips in search of a boyfriend. Surgical altering is a must for any intact Pug with a tendency to roam.

An open door is an invitation for your Pug to take off. Think about what your Pug sees every time she approaches the door. The door opens and she gets to go through it and into a great big world. It may mean access to the car for a ride or to the delivery man who always gives her a cookie. It might mean the beginning of a stroll through the neighborhood or that a friend is waiting outside. If your Pug exits the doorway without the safety of a leash she can get into a lot of trouble very quickly.

Doorway Boundaries

Teach your Pug at an early age that she is not to pass through a doorway unless she receives permission to do so. The *wait* command outlined in Chapter 7 is used to teach doorway boundaries.

Your Pug should be on leash for this training exercise. She can be standing or, preferably, in a sitting position to begin. Give the *wait* command and slowly begin to open the door. If your Pug moves forward toward the open door give a sharp leash correction by popping back (away

from the door) as you simultaneously close the door. She learns that movement not only causes a leash correction, it also makes the door close! Repeat this exercise several times each day until she reliably follows the *wait* command. At this point you can give her the release word and allow her to move forward with you through the door.

Continue to practice this exercise each day, increasing the amount of time that your Pug must wait until she hears the release word. Be prepared to close the door if she moves before then. Each time you open the door a little wider, she may be tempted to bolt without waiting for your command. Do not allow her to cheat! She must learn to wait for your cue.

Come Back

If your Pug does take off and run it is important that she *come* when she is called (see Chapter 7). Don't wait until she is off and running. It is never too early to start teaching your Pug how to *come* on command.

Quiet Please!— Silencing Barking

Barking is a normal form of communication for dogs. Unfortunately, some dogs bark at inappropriate times or to excess. When your Pug barks too much it can become a problem that is difficult to ignore.

The earlier you recognize inappropriate barking, the better the chance that you can correct it. When your Pug barks to let you know she has to eliminate, that barking behavior is appropriate. A short barking sequence in response to the doorbell is also appropriate. When your Pug barks because the wind blows or fails to quiet down in an appropriate length of time, the barking behavior is inappropriate.

Your Pug may bark because she is bored, anxious, or excited. It is important to try to find out what triggers the barking. If boredom is the cause, she must have something to do that keeps her stimulated. If she is nervous or scared, you must first try to determine what is making her anxious, and then make changes to her environment to make her more comfortable and secure. Separation anxiety may cause inappropriate barking when left alone.

Barking Basics

The earlier you teach your Pug how to stop barking on command, the easier it will be for her to learn the concept of *quiet*. Whenever you are dealing with inappropriate barking there are three steps that must be taken:

1. Interrupt the barking sequence.
2. Redirect to another activity.
3. Reward quiet, constructive behavior.

Each time your Pug starts a barking sequence, give the *quiet* command in a loud, stern tone of voice. As soon as she is quiet, praise her and then redirect her to some other behavior. Ask her to *sit* or find her a toy to play with. It is also beneficial to remove her from the stimulus if possible.

Barking behaviors can be some of the toughest to change. Interrupting the barking sequence without inadvertently

Pugs are not normally excessive barkers.

rewarding the dog can be a challenge. There are several different techniques that you can try when faced with inappropriate barking. First, you can try making a loud noise. Try dropping a book or slapping your hand on a tabletop. It is important that you do not scream or yell as your Pug may take this as a signal that you are trying to help her by making noise yourself.

There are several tools that you can use as interruption devices. Throw a shaker can in her direction. A jogger's air horn, used in short bursts to interrupt the barking, or a blast of water from a squirt gun may also be effective. There are also anti-barking collars, in both electronic shock and spray versions that can be exceptionally effective for curbing inappropriate barking.

Long-Term Management

If your Pug has a habit of barking to excess, or barking at even the slightest noise, it may take many months to change her behavior. If you are using an anti-bark collar, you should make sure that you continue to leave it on for an additional four to six weeks after she seems to be over her inappropriate barking behavior. It is important that you do not allow your Pug to intermittently bark inappropriately for any reason or she will begin to do so in a variety of situations.

Mounting

Mounting behavior among dogs is actually quite normal. When one dog mounts

another it can be part of play behavior or an attempt to gain social status or rank among dogs. When this behavior occurs between two dogs it is important to realize that they are communicating in a normal manner. Mounting only becomes an issue if a subordinate dog oversteps her boundaries by mounting a dominant dog and the dominant dog then feels the need to reassert himself. A confrontation or physical conflict may ensue until the subordinate dog submits to the more dominant dog.

Mounting behavior that is directed toward humans by a dog is a behavior that should not be tolerated. Mounting behavior is most often exhibited by young dogs, usually when they are maturing and trying to establish themselves in the family order. The most common targets of mounting behavior are toddlers and children who are easily accessible while playing on the floor. Adults may become targets of this behavior if they are not viewed as leaders.

If your Pug decides to try asserting herself by mounting it is important to stop this behavior quickly. You must interrupt this behavior by projecting yourself as more of a leader. If she begins to mount a child the child should stand up immediately and try to push the dog away. Better yet, minimize the time the child spends on the floor while your Pug is present. If her behavior is directed toward an adult, that person can try to be a bit more assertive in making the point that the behavior is inappropriate. A collar correction may be appropriate in this circumstance.

9 Canine Good Citizen Test and Therapy Dog Training

Every dog should be well-trained enough to walk in public without difficulty and greet people confidently and calmly. Pugs love to be in the spotlight and they often bring a smile to those around them. If you have spent time teaching your Pug how to properly behave in public, consider making him a Canine Good Citizen.

The Purpose

The American Kennel Club launched its Canine Good Citizen Test, or CGC, in 1989. The goal was to reward dogs exhibiting good manners both in public and in the home. The CGC test is non-competitive, demonstrating not only your Pug's ability to behave himself in a variety of situations, but your commitment to his health and well-being.

Benefits of a Canine Good Citizen

Owning a well-behaved Pug is personally satisfying, but there are other benefits too! The owner of a Pug with good manners rarely hears complaints from friends and family. Completion of the CGC test proves that your Pug is a good neighbor. Some insurance companies will even waive fees associated with dog ownership when the dog has a CGC certificate. Successfully passing the CGC test indicates that you have invested time and energy in your Pug's education. The work you do will provide a great foundation for any other avenue of training you wish to pursue.

The Testing Requirements

There is no age limit for the CGC test. Dogs of any age can pass the test as long as they have good manners. The American Kennel Club does encourage the owners of puppies under a year of age to have their dog retested after they reach adulthood. This proves that you have remained committed to training him as he grows and matures. The test is scored either "Pass" or "Needs More Training." Buckle collars and slip collars are the only collars allowed during the CGC test, and no food or treats may be used during the testing process. You are encouraged to praise your dog throughout the testing process, but corrections may result in a "Needs More Training" score, and you will need to retake the test at a later date.

The Canine Good Citizen Test is divided in two parts. First you will demonstrate your responsibility as a good dog owner, followed by ten exercises to prove your Pug is well behaved. You will be required to sign the Responsible Dog Owner's Pledge, attesting that your dog is current on vaccinations and has visited your veterinarian regularly. Then you are ready to take the test with your dog. A trained evaluator will instruct you through the testing process.

The CGC test is usually given in a very informal setting. If you have been attending obedience classes you will find that the process is run very similarly to an obedience class. All of the exercises will be performed with your Pug on leash.

Preparing for the Test

Prepare for the CGC test by exposing your Pug to a variety of situations and stimuli. The first step is to enroll him in a puppy kindergarten class, basic obedience class, or Canine Good Citizen class. The lessons learned in these environments will prepare your Pug for the items of the test that involve basic commands and self-control. You will gain the confidence to lead your Pug through all of the items on the test.

Practice by staging some of the exercises that involve meeting people or walking quietly through a crowd. Ask friends

or neighbors to help you, or try walking through town or in a local pet store. How does your Pug react? Is he looking at you for direction, or is he trying to be a "greeter" rushing up to everyone he sees? Once he can focus his attention on you regardless of the activity around him, he is ready to take the CGC test. For some Pugs an advanced beginner class may be needed before they are capable of sustaining the focus needed to perform well on the test.

Where to Test?

Canine Good Citizen tests are offered in nearly every part of the country by kennel clubs, obedience training clubs, veterinarians, and private dog trainers. You can find a CGC test near you by visiting the American Kennel Club's Web site at *www.akc.org/cgc*.

The CGC Test Items

Your Pug's manners will be evaluated using ten different exercises. He will need to receive a passing grade for all ten exercises in order to receive the Canine Good Citizen certificate.

Test 1: Accepting a Friendly Stranger

What Pug doesn't want to meet a friendly stranger? This test is designed to demonstrate that your Pug can accept a friendly approach from a stranger and behave while you carry on a conversation. He will not be able to engage in activity with the evaluator, show any signs of shyness during the interaction, or break position.

You can ask your Pug to *sit* and *stay* as you approach the evaluator, but he must remain in that position during this test. If you need to constantly correct your Pug during this exercise or use the leash to restrain him from greeting the tester, you will receive a Needs More Training rating.

Test 2: Sitting Politely for Petting

Pugs love physical contact! This exercise should be easy for your Pug to pass as long as he can exhibit self-control during the testing. The exercise begins in a sitting position on your side (*heel* position works great, as does *sit* or *stay*). You may talk to your Pug. The evaluator will ask if she can pet your dog and then gently pet him on the head and body. Your Pug may stand while he is petted, and may move forward slightly to receive more petting, but may not lunge or jump on the evaluator or attempt to move away from the physical contact. He must appear to be under your control during this exercise.

Test 3: Appearance and Grooming

This test demonstrates your Pug's willingness to accept an exam from someone such as a veterinarian or groomer, and demonstrates your commitment to keeping him healthy and well groomed. You may encourage your Pug throughout this test

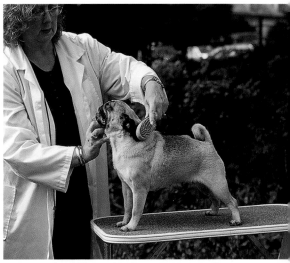

Your Pug should be trained to accept grooming and brushing.

and he does not have to remain in one position during the examination. The evaluator will pretend to examine your Pug and use a brush or comb (that you supply) to softly brush your Pug. The evaluator will then examine his ears by gently picking up each ear flap. Next, the feet will be examined. Pugs in general do not like to have their feet touched or held, so make sure that yours can tolerate this exercise without pulling away or struggling.

Test 4: Walking on a Loose Lead

This is a demonstration of your control during a brief walk. Your Pug may be on either side of you during the test and must continually demonstrate that he is paying attention to you and responding when you

A Pug that earns his CGC is a model canine citizen.

change direction. The "walk" pattern must contain at least one right turn, left turn, and about turn, and at least one stop while heeling. Your Pug does not have to sit when you stop in order to pass this exercise, but may not pull excessively or continually attempt to sniff the ground.

Test 5: Walking in a Crowd

This test demonstrates that your Pug can politely walk near a group of people. The test will consist of at least three people, (one of them may be a child), and there may be a dog that remains sitting in the crowd during the exercise. At least one person will be moving during the exercise.

You will be asked to walk your Pug near the group. He may show curiosity in the people, but must continue to walk with you at all times. He cannot pull away or try to jump on the people, but he may sniff individuals as you walk by.

Test 6: Sit and Down on Command and Stay in Place

If you have passed a basic obedience course there should be no problem in passing this portion of the test. You will be instructed to ask your Pug to respond to both a *sit* and a *down* command. Once he has successfully demonstrated that he knows these commands you can choose whether he is to *sit* and *stay* or *down* and *stay*. You will give him the *stay* command and walk approximately twenty feet in front of him. He must remain in the spot that you left him although he may stand up or sit up and still pass. You will be instructed to return to your Pug and he must remain in position until you give the release command. Your Pug will pass as long as he does not move toward you at any time during the exercise. If the CGC test is being given outdoors you will be asked to place your Pug on a twenty foot lead before beginning this test. You will be allowed to give the command to *sit* and *stay* more than once, but you may not force the dog into either position.

Test 7: Come When Called

This test will demonstrate that your Pug will return to you when called. He will still be on the twenty foot lead from Test 6. You may begin this exercise in any position. Give the command to *wait* or *stay*, or simply walk away from him. You will be asked to move to a spot approximately ten feet away, then turn and call the dog to you. It is permissible to use multiple signals such as voice commands, hand signals, or other body language cues in order to get your Pug to respond. If he moves toward you after you leave him, the evaluator may distract him as this exercise does not evaluate any other command except *come*. Your Pug must return to you within a reasonable amount of time once you have called him, and must return directly to you.

Test 8: Reaction to Another Dog

Once again if you have taken the time to complete a basic obedience class, your Pug should pass this test with flying colors. This test demonstrates that your Pug can approach a strange dog and handler with nothing more than casual interest. The dog and handler team will approach you and then stop to have a short conversation. Your dog must remain along your side during the conversation and may not attempt to engage, play with, or jump on the other dog. He may show casual interest such as sniffing. After shaking hands, the dog and handler will continue to walk past you. Your Pug may watch the team leave, but he may not turn and pull as if to follow them.

Test 9: Reaction to Distraction

This test is designed to show that your Pug is well adjusted and has had exposure to a variety of sights and sounds that might occur in everyday situations. Two different distractions will be used for each test. One will generally be a sound distraction, the other a sight distraction. Some of the common distractions that may be used are

- dropping a chair or pan, or opening or closing a door;
- a person riding a bicycle, in a wheelchair or walker, or jogging;
- opening or closing an umbrella;
- a person pushing a shopping cart or pulling a dolly.

Distractions in the CGC test may cause your Pug to tilt his head as if to say "What was that?"

demonstrate that your Pug can accept direction from a stranger and will remain well behaved during your absence. The test begins with a stranger asking if she can watch your dog. You will hand the leash to that person and walk to a designated position out of your Pug's sight. He does not have to remain in any one position, but must not whine excessively, bark, or show signs of anxiety or stress during the test. The stranger may talk to your dog, but she may not engage in any play activity. If the stranger is sitting in a chair during the test, your Pug may attempt to jump up on the stranger. The stranger's response will be to stand up.

Your Pug may react slightly to each distraction, showing curiosity or perhaps giving an initial startled response, but he should not panic, try to pull away, or bark more than once. Any sign of shyness, fear, or aggression will result in a Needs More Training mark for this test. You may give encouragement during this exercise. Use the *watch me* command to keep your Pug focused on you, not the distraction!

Test 10: Supervised Separation

The final test may be the most difficult. Your Pug will be left with a friendly stranger while you walk out of sight for three minutes. This exercise is designed to

From Good Citizen to Therapy Dog

In 1976, Elaine Smith, a registered nurse working in England, began to observe positive changes in those patients who were visited by the hospital chaplain and his Golden Retriever. Elaine returned to the United States with a plan to bring well-behaved dogs into health care facilities for therapy work. Therapy Dogs International, Inc. (TDI), was formed, bringing the concept of canine-assisted therapy into reality. TDI was the first organization to certify dogs for therapy work and maintain a list of qualified, volunteer handlers and their therapy dogs for health care professionals. Other organizations have been formed worldwide to bring canine-assisted therapy into many health care facilities as an adjunct form of therapy. A Canine Good Citizen certificate is the first step in attaining a Therapy Dog Certificate.

Therapy dogs are not service dogs or guide dogs. Although certification through one of the many therapy dog organizations may provide you with insurance, you will not be granted legal rights or the same protection as a service or assistance dog.

Benefits of a Therapy Dog

You already know how much happiness and joy your Pug brings to you on any given day. Why not share this with others? Certified therapy dogs visit nursing homes, hospitals, and other facilities, entertaining residents, providing companionship, and sometimes performing tricks for the patients. Researchers believe that these visits increase emotional awareness in many older patients and promote healing in some patients by helping to lower stress levels. Simply petting a dog can help to lower blood pressure, and canine-assisted therapy may make some residents who are depressed feel less despondent.

Therapy Dog Certification

Each therapy dog organization has its own set of requirements. Though the actual exercises may differ in name from one organization to the next, the general concepts for certification are similar. Passing the Canine Good Citizen test may exempt you from some of the testing requirements for some organizations. Some of the additional paperwork requirements are

- proof of current vaccinations
- proof of current veterinary examination
- proof of negative parasite status
- testing must be on a buckle collar or harness only

Additional testing requirements are designed to show that your Pug is comfortable around health care equipment. The following are the TDI requirements:

- **Reaction to medical equipment.** The dog must not be frightened by things commonly found in a hospital or nursing home. The equipment may be introduced in any of the following Canine Good Citizen tests: Test 2, Test 3, Test 5, or Test 9.
- **Leave It.** Your Pug must demonstrate that he will ignore items that may be on the ground or at his level.
- **Distractions associated with the infirm.** The dog must not overreact to people with an uneven gait, cough, wheeze, or spastic movements.
- **Say hello.** Your Pug must demonstrate that he can be well behaved and is willing to visit with anyone, especially children. He must tolerate petting and show no sign of fear or aggression.

10 *Rally Obedience*

Rally Obedience is a relatively new form of obedience competition. Rally competition combines traditional obedience exercises with the ability to interact and encourage your Pug through the course. Communication between dog and handler is not only allowed but encouraged in Rally Obedience. When competing in Rally Obedience you may talk to your Pug, clap your hands, pat your legs, or give other encouragement as you complete each exercise. Rally obedience has several levels of competition. Each level combines different exercises with the level of difficulty increasing as you compete at each level.

Competition Venues

Two different dog organizations offer competition in rally obedience. While the exercises used for competition are essentially the same in both venues, the rules for competition differ slightly between the two organizations.

APDT Rally-O

Many people credit the Association of Pet Dog Trainers (APDT) for introducing the sport of rally to the dog world. In 1998 Charles "Bud" Kramer began to develop a new form of obedience. He envisioned an obedience competition that paralleled training, one that allowed unlimited communication and encouragement from the owner during the course. The APDT began to offer rally-o as a competition in 2001, and the sport has grown steadily since then.

Rally competitions sanctioned by the APDT are open to all dogs, including mixed breeds. Dogs with disabilities are not only eligible, but encouraged to compete in APDT rally-o, as long as they do not exhibit any signs of pain or discomfort during the competition.

The APDT rules do not allow any type of correction collar to be used at events. Choke or slip collars, head halters, and "no pull" harnesses are all prohibited during competition. Buckle or flat collars and standard harnesses are allowed; the judge will visually inspect the collar.

Food rewards and physical touching are allowed in APDT competition. Food rewards must be hidden in a pocket and may only be given at the completion of some, but not all, exercises. Food rewards may not be given during heeling and may not interrupt a handler's ability to move continuously between exercises.

The position of the dog in relation to the handler is much more relaxed in APDT rally competition. If the dog is facing the same direction as the handler, is on the handler's left side, and the head is easily within reach, the dog is considered to be in the correct position.

AKC Rally

The American Kennel Club introduced rally obedience competition in 2005. This competition was well received by individuals not yet ready to compete in traditional obedience classes, and offered another chance for retired canine competitors to return to the ring.

AKC Rally competition is open to purebred dogs only. Pugs that are AKC registered are eligible for competition, as are Pugs able to obtain an ILP number from the American Kennel Club. Dogs with disabilities, however, are not eligible for AKC competition.

When competing in AKC rally obedience, neither food rewards nor physical contact is permitted. Buckle, slip, or choke collars are allowed, but prong-type collars are not. Proper *heel* position for AKC rally has the dog facing the same direction as the handler and positioned on the handler's left side.

The Rally Course

Each competition has a course designed by the judge. Individual exercises, known as "stations," must be completed in a specific order. The number of stations and the degree of difficulty of the course are determined by the level at which you and your Pug are competing.

Rally Signs

On every course, each station is numbered to make the sequence of the course easy to follow. Each station also has a sign explaining which exercise is to be performed. These signs include descriptions of the exercises as well as arrows for directional guidance. The signs are generally placed to the right of the handler. Unless otherwise specified by the sign, exercises should always be performed in close proximity to the sign. An exercise may be performed in front of, in back of, or beside the designated sign.

Stationary Exercises

Stationary exercises are those that involve a physical position change for the dog, while you remain still. When performing these exercises you can use hand signals and verbal cues in any combination to

---

PUG POINTER

An Indefinite Listing Privilege number given to dogs that do not have AKC registration papers, but are clearly recognizable as an AKC breed.

You may obtain an ILP number by submitting an ILP form to the American Kennel Club, along with two photographs of your Pug and a letter from your veterinarian verifying that your Pug has been surgically altered.

Focus is the key to successfully competing with your Pug.

Movement Exercises

Movement exercises make up the majority of the stations on a Rally course. A station may require that you and your Pug complete the station moving in unison or with the dog moving in an opposite direction and then rejoining you in moving forward. Some of these exercises can be quite intricate and complex, combining turns, circles, and pivots. There are even some stations that require the dog to navigate a jump or pass up a bowl of food without stopping to investigate it.

Some movement exercises that may be performed are right and left turns, 360-degree turn, slow and face pace, serpentine, weave once, left about turn, offset figure eight.

Levels of Competition

In both APDT rally-o and AKC rally there are three levels of competition. A dog must successfully complete each level three times before being allowed to compete in the next level. Upon completion of a level, the dog receives a letter designation after her name. The three levels of competition in APDT rally-o are designated as Level 1, Level 2, and Level 3. In AKC Rally these levels are called Novice, Advanced, and Excellent. Within each level, the competition is split into an "A" class, for dog and handler teams that have never earned the title for that level, and a "B" class, for teams that have earned the title, but have not moved up to the next level.

encourage your Pug to get the exercise right. Some examples of stationary exercises are halt/sit, halt/down, halt/sit/down, halt/fast forward from sit, call dog front/finish right forward.

Stationary exercises make up the smallest number of stations on any course. More advanced classes require a greater amount of movement from both dog and handler and include left about turn, halt/walk around dog, halt/turn right one step/call to heel/halt.

Level 1—Novice

When competing for the first time dogs are entered in the Level 1 class for rally-o or the Novice class for AKC rally. The exercises in both competition venues are to be performed on leash at this level. Rally-o offers bonus exercises that may be performed off leash or with the dog dragging the leash.

In rally-o the Level 1 course has eighteen to twenty stations. In AKC Rally, the course has ten to fifteen stations, with no more than five of these stations involving stationary exercises. When your Pug successfully completes three courses with "Qualifying Scores" an RL1 designation (rally-o), or RN title (AKC obedience) is awarded.

Level 2—Advanced

The second level of competition is always performed off leash. The exercises are more complex and the dog must pay close attention to you in order to successfully navigate the course as a team. A Level 2 course consists of twenty to twenty-two exercises. Bonus exercises are also offered. In the Advanced class, you can expect twelve to seventeen stations. Stationary exercises will make up no more than seven stations at the advanced level. Jumps are also required as part of the Level 2 and Advanced competition. The titles earned at this level are RL2 (rally-o) and RA (AKC).

Level 3—Excellent

The final level of competition is the most difficult. The exercises are complex and require a great deal of teamwork in order to successfully navigate the course and receive a qualifying score. All work is done off leash. The Level 3 exercises combine jumps with turns; bonus exercises involve retrieving a specific object. There are twenty to twenty two stations in a rally-o Level 3 course. In AKC competition exercises include backing up three steps as a team and a moving stand. AKC rally also offers a bonus exercise at this level known as the "honor" exercise. This is either a *sit* or *down* and *stay* in a designated location within the competition ring, while the next team completes the course. There are fifteen to twenty stations in an AKC rally course, with no more than seven stationary exercises. A RL3 title or an RE title can be earned by successfully completing three courses with a qualifying score.

Competing in Rally

Competing with your Pug in Rally Obedience can be a fun pastime for both of you. Before you will be ready to enter your first trial you will need to commit to some hard work, remaining dedicated to training every day.

Rally Classes

One of the best ways to begin preparing for competition is to enroll in a rally class. These are often offered through local kennel clubs, dog kennels, or dog obedience schools.

A good rally class will help you identify each sign and explain how the exercise is supposed to be performed. The instructor may also give you information on local trials. You should plan to attend a rally trial and observe dog and handler teams as they move through the course.

Rally Run-throughs

A mock rally trial is called a run-through or fun match. A run-through gives you the opportunity to practice an actual rally course, complete with a judge, but without the pressure of competing for your title. Attending a fun match can be a great tune up before you enter a trial for the first time. Rally fun matches are often offered by larger training groups or kennel clubs.

Walk Throughs

You will no doubt be nervous the first time you compete at an actual trial. Don't worry! Other competitors are nervous too. You will have an opportunity before your class starts to actually walk the course without your Pug, to familiarize yourself with the stations and how the course flows. Take your time and don't be afraid

---

PUG POINTER

For more information on rules and regulations of rally competition visit

The Association of Pet Dog Trainers (www.apdt.com)

The American Kennel Club (www.akc.org)

---

to repeat the course several times during the walk through session.

Scoring

Scoring for a rally trial is not as strict as a regular obedience trial. In APDT rally-o there is a possible score of 200 points. In AKC rally the highest score possible is 100 points. Deductions are based on the severity of mistake or fault. The minimum deduction in rally is one point. The maximum deduction for a single exercise is ten points.

Some faults and their average deductions are

One Point	Three Points	Ten Points
Tight leash	Repeat of a station	Incorrectly performing a station
Poor sits	Lack of control	
Slow response		
	Harsh/loud commands	

A major fault or mistake may result in a non-qualifying score or NQ. If your Pug is not under control, is barking throughout the course, or leaves the ring before the course is finished, the judge will score the performance as non-qualifying. A qualifying score in APDT rally-o is 170 points or more. In AKC rally competition you will receive a qualifying score for 70 points or higher. A qualifying score is also known as a "leg."

11 *Traditional Obedience*

Traditional obedience competitions have been the mainstay of companion events for many years. Competing in obedience is challenging, but there is nothing more rewarding to watch than a handler and her dog working together with precision. Traditional obedience competitions combine all of the basic obedience commands discussed in Chapter 8 with heeling patterns, both on and off leash. Advanced classes in obedience also contain exercises that involve jumping and retrieving.

body language, and corrections or multiple cues or signals are penalized. Scoring is based upon the number of errors or faults; deductions can range from one-half of one point up to ten points. A non-qualifying score can also be given for major errors or for failure to complete an exercise.

A perfect score in obedience competition is 200 points. A qualifying score, or leg, is a score of 170 points or higher. Earn three legs in any division and you and your Pug receive a title for that division.

Introduction to Competition

In 1933, Helen Whitehouse Walker developed an obedience "test" to demonstrate the intelligence of her poodles. The American Kennel Club offered its first licensed obedience trial in 1936.

The AKC offers obedience trials as a way for dogs and owners to demonstrate precision and teamwork. When competing, dog and handler teams are judged based on a theoretical "perfect" performance that the judge has mentally pictured. Unlike a rally trial you cannot encourage your Pug throughout the course. During all exercises, communication is mainly through

Practice Makes Perfect

In dog obedience, daily practice is an essential part of becoming a team. Training your Pug to be well behaved at home took time and patience. Training for obedience competition is like training for the Olympics! But if you commit the time and train in a positive manner, you will find that your Pug thoroughly enjoys the bond that will develop between the two of you.

Obedience Classes

If you are considering competing, your first step must be to enroll in a basic obedience class. An eight-week obedience class will help your Pug learn to perform around the distractions of other dogs and will help you learn to control your Pug when there are other dogs present. Before you can even consider competition, your Pug must learn to maintain focus on you no matter what is going on around him. He must also be willing to work with you in spite of the temptation of other dogs interacting so close to him.

After the successful completion of a beginner obedience class you must continue training by enrolling in an advanced beginner class. Advanced beginner classes typically focus on teamwork, increasing time and distance for each exercise, and begin to create the foundation for off-leash heeling.

Some training facilities and kennel clubs offer classes specifically designed for those dogs and their owners interested in competition obedience. There is no substitution for working your Pug in a competition class! The instructors are often serious obedience competitors themselves and they have the skill and the knowledge to help you and your Pug achieve success in the obedience ring.

Obedience Matches

An obedience match is another way to practice the exercises without actually entering an obedience trial. It is important to note that there are two types of obedience matches: sanctioned matches and correction matches.

Competing in a sanctioned match is quite similar to competing in an obedience trial. The judge will instruct you in the same manner as in an obedience trial. While you may give verbal corrections (which will result in a deduction), physical corrections are generally not allowed. You will not be allowed to repeat any exercise.

Correction matches allow you to give both verbal and physical corrections. The judge in most correction matches runs the ring as if it were an obedience trial, but if time permits you are allowed to repeat exercises. In some correction matches the judge will score the exercises, while in others the judge is merely there to simulate an obedience trial environment.

Obedience Trials

With many hours of practice under your belt the day will come when you are ready to compete. Obedience trials can be offered as a stand-alone event, where the only classes offered are for obedience, or they may be a part of an all-breed dog show.

If you have competed in rally obedience you may not be as nervous your first time entering the ring. Traditional obedience is a bit more nerve-racking because you have limited ability to communicate with your Pug in the ring. Take a deep breath before you enter and remember that both you and your Pug must exhibit a willingness to work together in order to succeed.

The Competition Classes

The first level you will compete at is the Novice class. With the exception of the group exercises, all of the Novice-level exercises are performed while the dog is on leash. When your Pug has earned three qualifying scores in Novice competition he will earn the title of Companion Dog or C.D.

The second level of competition is the Open class. Your Pug will perform all of the Open class exercises while off leash. Exercises are more complicated and require a great deal of training and practice to master. Three qualifying scores at the Open class level earn the Companion Dog Excellent or C.D.X. title.

The third level is the most difficult. The Utility class is the highest individual level of competition, and all of the exercises are done off leash. The Utility class may require several years of practice, and the exercises may be quite challenging for both you and your Pug to master. Earning the title of Utility dog, or U.D., means that your Pug is among the elite canine competitors in obedience.

Dogs must learn to perform for both hand signals and verbal commands. In the Novice and Open classes you may use verbal cues. These may be combined with a hand signal for some exercises, but not all. In Utility, your Pug must perform solely on hand signals for some exercises.

Class Divisions

Obedience classes are divided into two divisions, "A" and "B." In the Novice class the "A" division is for dog and handler teams that have never earned the title of C.D. The "B" division is for those owners who have previously shown in the Novice class and earned a C.D. Once you have earned a C.D. on one dog you are then required to compete in the "B" class with your next dog.

The "A" class in both Open and Utility are for dog and handler teams that have not earned a title. Earning a C.D.X. or U.D. on your Pug now does not mean your next obedience dog must compete in the "B" class. The "B" class in both Open and Utility is for those teams wishing to compete for advanced obedience titles.

Advanced Competition Titles

Is your Pug's obedience career over once he has earned the Utility Dog title? Absolutely not! There are several advanced competition titles that can be earned by simply continuing to compete and earn qualifying scores in both the Open "B" and Utility "B" classes.

- **Utility Dog Excellent (UDX)** Your Pug can earn this title once he has achieved the U.D. title by qualifying in both Open "B" and Utility "B" at ten separate trials.
- **Obedience Trial Champion (OTCH)** Considered to be the most difficult achievement for even the most willing obedience Pug, the OTCH can be earned by accumulating 100 points, and must include at least one first place win in both Open "B" and Utility "B," and a third first place win in either class. Points are awarded for placing first through fourth in either class and wins must be awarded by three different judges.
- **Versatile Companion Dog (VCD)** This title can be earned by competing and earning titles in both traditional obedience trials and agility trials.

Home Schooling

Novice Exercises

The Novice exercises show that your Pug can perform basic obedience skills.

Heel on Leash and Figure 8. These exercises are used to show the teamwork between the dog and handler. Fast and slow changes in pace are combined with left turns, right turns, and about turns. You will also be asked to *halt*. Your Pug must remain in *heel* position as you slow down and sit quickly in *heel* position when you stop. The Figure 8 exercise

Practicing obedience every day is the best way to overcome distractions.

combines circles to both the left and the right, in a heeling pattern around two individuals serving as posts. Scoring is based on 40 possible points.

Stand for Examination. The purpose of this exercise is to demonstrate that your Pug can stand when instructed, remain in the standing position, and tolerate a quick examination without displaying shyness or excitement. This exercise is done off leash. You will be asked to command your Pug to *stand* and *stay*, as you then walk to a designated spot approximately six feet in front and turn to face him. The judge will approach your Pug and "examine" him by touching his head, back, and hindquarters. You will then be allowed to return to your Pug by walking around him and back into *heel* position. Scoring is based on 30 possible points.

Heel Free. The Heel Free exercise is the same pattern as the Heel on Leash. Your Pug will be off leash however. There is no off leash Figure 8 exercise in the Novice class. Scoring is based on 40 possible points.

Recall/Finish. This exercise shows that your Pug will remain sitting in a designated spot and come directly to you when called. The exercise begins with your dog in *heel* position. You will be asked to *leave your dog* and walk to the other side of the ring. Upon the judge's signal or command you will be asked to *call your dog*. You may give a hand signal and a verbal command for *come*. Your Pug must come directly to you at a brisk pace and sit directly in front of you, close enough so that you can easily touch his head without excessively stretching out or moving your feet. Upon the command *finish* your Pug must move from sitting in front of you back into *heel* position, either by moving around and behind you or by moving to his right (your left) and swinging back into *heel* position. Scoring for this exercise is based on 30 possible points.

Long Sit. This demonstrates your Pug's ability to remain in position until you return to him. You will be asked to leave the dog and walk to the other side of the ring for a period of one minute. At the end of one minute you will return to your Pug by walking around him and back into *heel* position. Scoring is based on 30 possible points.

Long Down. This is often a Pug's best exercise. It demonstrates your Pug's ability to remain lying in position (often snoozing) until you return to him. The Long Down is performed exactly the same as the Long Sit exercise, except the length of time increases to three minutes. A perfect score in this exercise is 30 points.

Open Exercises

The Open exercises demonstrate your Pug's ability to perform more complicated patterns and tasks.

Heel Free and Figure 8. This exercise is exactly the same as the Novice Heel Free and Figure 8 except the leash is left with the ring attendant, before the start of the exercises. A perfect score for this exercise is 40 points.

Drop on Recall. This begins in the same manner as the Novice Recall, but your Pug will be asked to drop into a *down* position as he approaches you. The judge will instruct you to *call your dog* and then to *down your dog*, either verbally or by giving you a signal. Your Pug must drop immediately upon your command or signal, wait until you call him to you, and then come directly to you and sit in front of you. He must also return to *heel* position when instructed. This exercise is worth 30 points.

Retrieve on Flat. Your Pug must demonstrate the ability to wait in *heel* position while you throw a dumbbell, move briskly and directly to the dumbbell and pick it up when instructed, and bring it immediately back to you. Upon his return to you he must sit in front of you and hold the dumbbell until you give him the okay to release it. He must then return to *heel* position. This exercise is worth 20 points.

Retrieve Over High Jump. Similar to the Retrieve on Flat, your Pug will have to pick up a dumbbell with the added difficulty of jumping. You will begin with the dog in *heel* position. You will be asked to throw the dumbbell over a jump and then be instructed to send your Pug over the jump. He must successfully clear the jump, go directly to the dumbbell and pick it up, and bring it back to you by again clearing the jump. As in the Retrieve on Flat, your Pug must hold the dumbbell upon his return until instructed to release it, and then return to *heel* position when given the command to *finish*. This exercise is worth 30 points.

Broad Jump. This is a test of your Pug's staying power and jumping skill, using a telescoping jump consisting of four white boards (although your Pug may only be required to jump three boards). The dog must remain sitting in front of the jump while you move to the right and face the side of the jump. Upon your command he must jump straight over the jump and while he is in mid-air you must turn in position one-quarter turn to your right. Upon clearing the jump your Pug must immediately turn and come to you, and then sit in front of you. He must then return to *heel* position when commanded to do so. This exercise is worth 20 points.

Long Sit. This is similar to the Long Sit exercise in Novice. The difference is that the position must be held for three minutes and you will leave the ring and remain out of your Pug's sight. The exercise is worth 30 points.

Long Down. This is similar to the Long Down exercise in the Novice class. The time for remaining in the *down* position increases to five minutes (your Pug may take a nap) and you will again leave the ring and remain out of sight. The Long Down is also worth 30 points.

Utility Exercises

Competing in this class demonstrates incredible teamwork, focus, and communication. The exercises are challenging and include:

Signal Exercise. This exercise demonstrates your Pug's ability to recognize and correctly perform exercises based solely on non-verbal signals from you. An off-lead heeling pattern will begin this exercise. At some point during the heeling pattern the judge will give you the command to *stand your dog* and *leave your dog.* Both commands must be given with hand signals only as you are not allowed to verbally communicate with your Pug at any time during this exercise. You will move to the other end of the ring and turn to face your Pug. Upon the judge's signal you will give the command to *down,* followed by *sit,* and finally *come.* Your Pug must sit directly in front of you and return to *heel* position upon your hand signal. This exercise requires constant focus from the dog and clearly communicated signals from you. The exercise is worth a total of 40 points.

Scent Discrimination. This is a difficult exercise for many Pugs. The dog must be able to find your scent on an article, or a leather or metal dumbbell, set among eight additional articles. The judge will ask you to pick one article of each type and place it on a chair. The remaining articles will be placed on the floor approximately 20 feet behind you. You will have a short amount of time to rub the first article with your hands. After the judge places the article among the other articles you will be told to turn and send your Pug to find the one with your scent. The exercise will be repeated with the second article. This exercise is worth 30 points per article, for a total of 60 points.

Directed Retrieve. This demonstrates your Pug's ability to follow a hand signal to a specific glove, pick up the glove, and return it to you. This exercise is difficult to execute, as at the start you will have your back to the gloves and the dog in *heel* position. You must both turn in sync to face the specified glove and your Pug must sit immediately in *heel* position. Your Pug must wait until you give the hand signal and verbal command to retrieve the glove. Any deviation from the glove specified will result in a deduction of points. The exercise is worth 30 points.

Moving Stand for Examination. This exercise is similar to the Stand for Examination in Novice. The level of difficulty is increased, as the exercise begins with a heeling pattern. The judge will give the command to s*tand your dog* and he must immediately stop, stand, and remain in place as you continue to walk forward approximately ten to twelve feet. The judge will then examine him. This exercise differs from previous competition levels in that you will be asking your Pug to come to you and move directly into *heel* position instead of stopping in front of you. This element of the Moving Stand makes it the only exercise that does not require the dog to return to the front, something he has been doing repeatedly in previous exercises and competition. The Moving Stand is worth another 30 points.

Directed Jumping. This is one of the most difficult exercises to train for. It involves sending your Pug away from you

A Pug sails over the high jump in an obedience competition.

to the opposite end of the ring, teaching him to turn to face you, and commanding him to *sit*. There are two jumps, the bar jump and the high jump, one on each side of the ring. Upon your command your Pug must jump over the correct jump and return to you by sitting in front of you. The exercise will be repeated, but this time the dog will have to jump the opposite jump. To successfully pass this exercise your Pug must be focused and confident. The total number of points possible for this exercise is 40.

12 *Agility Competition*

Agility is the fastest growing dog sport in the United States. Pugs, once thought of as slow, lazy, and unenthusiastic competitors, have shown the world that they can run with the big dogs.

History

The concept of agility actually came about as an entertainment event at England's Crufts dog show in 1978. Peter Lewis, along with others, took concepts from equestrian events and created a jumping course to demonstrate how agile and quick dogs could be. Military dog training obstacles may have played a role in designing many of the current agility obstacles.

By the mid-1980s, dog trainers and obedience competitors in the United States began to take notice of the sport of agility and its popularity in England. The latter half of that decade saw the formation of the National Committee for Dog Agility (NCDA), the United States Dog Agility Association (USDAA), and the North American Dog Agility Council (NADAC). The NCDA merged with the United Kennel Club (UKC) in 1994. In that same year, the American Kennel Club held its first sanctioned agility event. The sport has enjoyed increasing popularity ever since.

Agility Trials

Agility trials are held virtually every week in nearly every area of the country. Agility competition pits a dog-and-handler team against a series of obstacles and the clock. The obstacle course must be completed within a specified amount of time and in a precise order. The handler guides the dog through the course, without the use of a leash, by communicating through hand signals, verbal commands, and lots of practice. Completion of the course after the Standard Course Time (SCT) will result in penalties. Touching the dog or any of the obstacles during the course is a disqualification. No food or training aids may be used in competition.

Scoring is based on how many faults a team has, combined with the fastest times. Similar to equestrian show jumping, faults are assessed for a dog that hits or knocks down a jump. Faults are also assessed for missing a contact zone, failing to follow the proper sequence of obstacles, or refusing an obstacle.

Agility Trial Classes

Agility trial classes can be somewhat confusing to the new competitor. Each agility organization has its own set of classes, and within those classes, different divisions. The American Kennel Club offers two types of classes: the Standard Class and the Jumpers with Weaves Class. The obstacles for each class are

Standard Class
- Dog Walk
- A-Frame
- See-saw
- Pause Table
- Weave Poles
- Open and Closed Tunnels
- Bar Jumps (single and double)
- Panel Jump
- Tire Jump
- Broad Jump

Jumpers with Weaves
- Weave Poles
- Open and Closed Tunnels
- Bar Jumps (single and double)
- Panel Jump
- Tire or Window Jump
- Triple Bar Jump

The North American Dog Agility Council has a larger offering of classes. The obstacles used in NADAC competition are

- Dog Walk
- Hoops
- Hoopgates
- Weave Poles
- Directional Hoops
- Non-Winged Jumps
- A-Frame

- Winged Jumps
- Open Tunnel

When competing in NADAC sanctioned events you have the choice of entering in the following classes

- Regular
- Jumpers
- Tunnelers
- Weavers
- Touch 'N Go
- Chances
- Hoopers
- Gaters

The United States Dog Agility Association uses the following obstacles

- A-Frame
- See-saw
- Dog Walk
- Weave Poles
- Pipe Tunnel
- Collapsible Tunnel
- Pause Table
- Tire Jump
- Three-winged Hurdles

You may compete in the following classes in USDAA competition

- Regular
- Gamblers
- Jumpers
- Relay
- Snooker

Class Divisions

The class divisions for agility can vary significantly among the agility organizations. Some organizations divide classes based on the age of the dog; others offer classes based solely on the age of the handler. Most, if not all, divide each class by the competitive skill level within the specific class. Dogs that have not previously achieved a title in agility generally compete in the Novice class division. As a dog successfully competes, receives qualifying scores and her title for the Novice class, she moves into the Open class level. Dogs that attain titles at the Open class division move into the more advanced Excellent or Elite levels. The number of obstacles used on a course increases with each skill level.

The height of a dog can also be a determination of class division. The height of a dog at the withers is measured and is recorded by a representative of the organization. The height determines which class division a dog should be entered in. The height divisions determine the height of the jumps in each class and may influence the Standard Course Time as well.

Obstacles

Although the names of the obstacles may vary slightly among the organizations, the types used are very similar. Each obstacle is built to a uniform standard within that organization. These obstacles, although challenging, are designed and built with the safety of the dog in mind. The way a dog enters or approaches an obstacle, the specific target areas she must touch, and the way a dog exits are all created to ensure that when executed properly, the safety of the dog is not jeopardized. When teaching your Pug about the obstacles, each should be given its own, unique name—a verbal clue to distinguish one obstacle from the next.

PUG POINTER

With the variations among agility organizations, their many different class types and divisions, your success will largely depend on your familiarization with the rules and regulations that apply to each organization. Before you begin to compete, you should obtain a rules and regulations booklet directly from the organization offering the trials in which you intend to compete, and read the rules prior to entering the trial. If you do not understand a rule, make sure that you contact the organization for clarification prior to your first trial date.

The pause table, the dog walk, the A-frame, and the see-saw are all known as contact obstacles. Contact obstacles require that the dog either touch a specific area, known as a contact zone, or perform some other task, such as a *sit* or *down*, while on the obstacle. Some contact obstacles are stationary, while others move as the dog maneuvers along the obstacle.

There are two types of tunnels used in agility competition. Open tunnels have wide openings at both ends. Some may be straight giving the dog a view from one end to the other, while others are bent or curved, making the obstacle more challenging. Collapsible or closed tunnels generally have on open end for the dog to enter the obstacle while the far end collapses until the dog exits the chute.

Weave poles are stationary vertical poles that the dog must learn to navigate. By entering the obstacle with the first pole to her left, and then weaving in and out of the subsequent poles, your Pug should be able to negotiate this obstacle quickly. The number of poles used increases from six poles in the Novice division to nine to twelve poles in the more advanced divisions.

Jumps vary greatly among the different agility organizations. Some of the jump courses are quite elaborate, mirroring the equestrian show jumping courses. There are jumps that lie flat on the ground, jumps with single or multiple bars, and jumps with wings. In some courses your Pug may have to negotiate jumping through a tire suspended by chains or a jump that simulates a window.

Preparing Your Pug for Competition

Weave in, weave out.

When you think about running your Pug in agility you should envision a dynamic duo! The sport requires that the two of you work continuously as a team in order to be successful. Your Pug must be under your control at all times even though you have no leash with which to communicate. At times, your Pug may be working at a significant distance from you.

Home Preparation

While you may not be able to set up an entire agility course in your backyard, there are steps that you can take to help your Pug train for an agility career. First you should expose her to a variety of objects as early as possible. Walking on different surfaces, from brick sidewalks to wooden bridges, will help her experience the sensation each produces. Children's play equipment can also be a great way for your Pug to experiment with obstacles. (Make sure that you follow the rules if you plan to use a public playground.) Toy stores are a great source for inexpensive, Pug-sized obstacles. You might also consider purchasing some agility equipment for training at home. There are many dog supply companies that offer well-constructed agility obstacles for sale at reasonable prices.

Next, you will want to make sure that you have worked on your Pug's ability to focus on you in hectic places. An agility trial can be very noisy, full of dogs that are ready and raring to go. If your Pug is

PUG POINTER

Part of your home preparation for your Pug is to make sure that she is mentally and physically fit. Working in agility is very demanding and your Pug must be in top condition in order to excel. Here are some ways to help your Pug meet the demands of agility.

- *Make sure that she is at the proper weight. Too much weight puts strain on the joints and may contribute to muscle pulls and ligament strains.*
- *Feed a high-quality diet that meets her increased caloric needs.*
- *Have your Pug examined by your veterinarian before you begin to jump her regularly. Proper joint conformation is important, as is normal vision.*
- *Agility should be fun! Try to teach obstacles in a positive manner.*
- *Never force your Pug to approach or attempt an obstacle if she is scared or nervous.*

not used to working under these conditions, competing in agility will be difficult for both of you.

Group Preparation

The best way to prepare for an agility career is to enroll in an Agility class. Working this way will introduce both of you to each obstacle. Research agility classes in your area and inquire if the instructors are also Agility competitors. Learning to work an Agility course takes time, energy, and effort. If the instructors are also seasoned competitors, they have a working knowledge of the rules for competition, and have experience in ring procedure. A good Agility instructor will not only teach you the proper way to signal your Pug to approach each obstacle, but will also help her become confident as she conquers each one. If your Pug is hesitant or unsure of herself, an Agility class provides a controlled setting that allows you to concentrate on those obstacles that may give your Pug a little trouble.

Motivating Your Pug

One of the quickest ways to introduce obstacles to an aspiring agility Pug is with small pieces of food. Most Pugs will willingly follow a food trail up to an obstacle. If you have been vigilant in exposing your Pug to a variety of obstacles and surfaces, there should be little hesitation in investigating food placed on or near the contact zones.

Some instructors like to teach the obstacles backwards. Take the A-frame, for example. To begin teaching your Pug how to climb it, widen the angle to make it less steep on the incline and descent. Instead of trying to make your Pug approach, climb, and descend the A-frame all at once, place a food treat in the contact zone on the descending side of the A-frame. Place your Pug at the bottom of the descending side of the A-frame and encourage her to calmly move off the obstacle to get the food reward. Repeat the exercise over and over, to increase your Pug's confidence, slowly moving her higher up the A-frame each time. Food rewards may be placed

Your enthusiasm on the agility course will help motivate your Pug.

on the A-frame as she is moves higher up the descending side. Eventually your Pug should be placed at the top of the ascending side, learning to move over the top of the A-frame and down the opposite side. As she becomes more proficient she will eagerly approach and conquer the A-frame and the angle will be reduced to slowly make it steeper.

Verbal encouragement is also used to motivate along the Agility course. Use high-pitched tones of voice, get excited, and let your Pug know that you are pleased with her progress on the obstacles. The more you talk to your dog and give prompts and signals on the course, the better your teamwork becomes. Remember, Pugs are born to be clowns and love to be the center of attention. When you display excitement during an Agility course the excitement can be contagious! Spectators may begin to get involved, offering cheers and applause, giving your Pug a reason to be a star.

13 Conformation Competition

Conformation is the "beauty pageant" of the dog world. The American Kennel Club, the Canadian Kennel Club, and the United Kennel Club all hold dog shows that feature conformation events. The first organized dog shows were held in England in the mid 1800s. The American Kennel Club was formed in 1884 and soon became the sanctioning body for conformation shows in the United States. The conformation show allows serious breeders to evaluate their dogs, selecting only those that are the best examples for breeding. Most strive to breed only those dogs that are exemplary representatives of their breed.

The blueprint for the perfect Pug describes the ideal Pug head as round. The body should be square, and the tail curled tightly on the back or over the hip. The standard also describes the Pug's feet, shoulders, legs, coat, and even how he should move.

At a conformation competition, a judge has the responsibility of looking at each Pug and determining how closely he conforms to the published breed standard. The judge will ask the dogs to move around a ring and stand on a table for an individual examination. The Pug that most closely fits the judge's mental picture of the perfect breed example will be the winner.

Breed Standard

Each breed has a published breed standard that acts as a blueprint, outlining what the perfect specimen of that particular breed should look like. The standard for the Pug, written by the Pug Dog Club of America and adopted by the American Kennel Club, defines what the perfect Pug head, body, and movement look like. Similarly, the Pug Dog Club of Canada has created a standard that is used by the Canadian Kennel Club.

Breed Championship

A breed champion is a dog that has competed in conformation shows and won enough times to meet the requirements of the kennel club for the championship certificate.

Points

In AKC conformation competition a dog must attain fifteen points in order to receive a championship. The number of

Not every Pug is born to compete in conformation.

points awarded at any show is based on the number of dogs actually competing at that show, and the region of the country the dog is being shown in. The highest number of points available at any one show is five. Wins that are awarded three, four, or five points are known as majors. Of the fifteen points necessary for a championship, two wins must be majors awarded by two different judges.

Points are only awarded to one male dog and one female, or bitch, of each breed, at each show. The winners of each class within the same sex compete against each other in the Winners class. The points winner at a show is called the "Winner's Dog" or "Winner's Bitch."

The Winner's Dog and Winner's Bitch will compete against all of the conformation champions that are entered in the show for the Best of Breed award. The Best of Breed class is the only class where both sexes compete against one another. Champions of record that continue to compete in conformation shows are also called "specials." Not every dog finishing a conformation championship goes on to become a special. The dog that wins Best of Breed goes on to compete with the other Best of Breed winners within their group. For Pugs, this is the Toy Group. Each group winner competes for the title of Best in Show.

Selecting a Conformation Pug

Not every Pug is born to be a beauty pageant winner. There are some special requirements that must be met before a dog can enter a conformation show. In order to be eligible for competition your Pug must be registered with the American Kennel Club in the United States, or the Canadian Kennel Club in Canada. His papers must be full-registration status; dogs sold as pets on limited registration are not eligible for conformation competition. Registration papers from other registering organizations are not accepted.

Next, your Pug must appear to meet the published breed standard as closely as possible. Your Pug may be beautiful and nearly perfect to you, but he must give this impression to a judge. The reality is that the vast majority of Pugs do not appear to meet most of the qualifications of the breed standard.

Neutered or surgically altered dogs are ineligible for conformation competition. The original purpose of the conformation show was to evaluate breeding stock. With this in mind, your Pug must be at least six months of age before he can be entered in a conformation show.

So how do you know if your Pug has what it takes to make it in the conformation ring?

1. Was he purchased from a show breeder? Purchasing a show prospect puppy from someone who is knowledgeable about the breed standard is one way to start off in the right direction.
2. Read the breed standard. Do you understand the terminology? Can you evaluate your Pug in a fair and impartial manner?
3. Attend a conformation show. Watch the Pugs that are entered and visualize the breed standard. How does your Pug measure up to the other Pugs in the ring?
4. Ask a show breeder to evaluate your Pug. The opinion of other people who know the breed may help you make an educated decision.

Your Pug may not have the right substance, body type, or features to make him competitive in the show ring, but that doesn't mean you should love him any less. He can still excel in companion animal events such as obedience or rally, or start training for agility competition or begin working toward becoming a therapy dog. Remember that a very small percentage of Pugs have all of the attributes to make it as a show dog.

Getting Started

The first thing to do if you are interested in showing in conformation is to attend a local dog show. This will allow you to see how a show operates and watch the other Pugs in competition. You will get to experience how chaotic a dog show can be and take in all the noise and the smells that accompany the event. These are all things that your Pug must learn to get used to while performing to the best of his ability.

Training for Conformation

Once you've decided that your Pug has the right stuff to compete in conformation, there are three things he will need to learn to do before he ever enters the show ring. He will have to learn to stand still, move around the ring at the proper pace, and stand on the table for the judge's examination. While these activities do not sound like they would be difficult to master, they can be tricky to teach. Many kennel clubs offer conformation classes that mimic the events that occur in a show ring. Your Pug must be allowed to experience what it is like to be elevated off of the ground in a strange location. He will need to learn to tolerate a stranger's hands as they examine his mouth, ears, body, and legs. Attending a conformation class should be the first step in training. The ring procedure at each show is pretty consistent and the more your Pug repeats the same scenario the more comfortable he'll be.

Gaiting

When you see show dogs parading around the ring at the end of a lead they are showing off their movement for the judge. You will need to teach your Pug to move at the correct speed. This is known as gaiting. While the correct speed for each dog is different, your Pug should be on your left side, moving at a steady pace that keeps his back level when gaiting. You must try to move in a straight line whenever you gait.

Your Pug must learn not to pull on the end of the leash as he gaits around the ring. Doing so changes the movement that the judge sees. One way to start this training is to teach him how to find *heel* position by using the technique in Chapter 6. Another option is to change direction whenever your Pug strays too far out in front of you during practice. He will be unable to anticipate which direction you may be heading and will quickly learn to pay attention to your leg movements instead of forging ahead. Don't forget to praise him if he's in the right spot.

Standing Still

Your Pug must learn to stand motionless in one position with his weight equally distributed over all four legs. Teaching him to walk into the proper standing position is called "free baiting" and it takes a lot of practice for a dog to learn to do well.

Start by teaching your Pug to associate the *stand* command with freezing in position. You can also use the *wait* command described in Chapter 8. Think of a hand signal that you will want to use with this command. You can begin teaching this exercise off leash. Give the command and hand signal and patiently wait until he stands still. As soon as he stops moving give a verbal reward and a food treat. When you are in the conformation ring you can use food rewards as long as they do not interfere with the judge's ability to examine your dog. Once your Pug knows that the command means to freeze, start working with him when he has his show lead on. The leash can be used as a tool to help him stop, move up, or move back. If your Pug is standing but has one front foot positioned slightly behind the other, gently pulling forward on the lead will send a signal to move the foot forward. Pull gently backwards on the lead and it signals a stop, or continued pressure backwards encourages him to move back. You should now only begin rewarding him when he is standing with his weight evenly distributed.

You may want to also teach your Pug to tolerate being positioned while in the *stand*. By kneeling down next to him and placing each leg squarely under his body, you can teach your Pug to assume that position each time he is told to *stand*. In the show ring, this is called "hand stacking." Hand stacking allows you to change the way your Pug looks to the judge if he is not able to stand correctly himself. It is also the procedure you will use to place your Pug on the table for his examination.

Standing still is tough for a Pug.

Table Presentation

The table presentation is done to give the judge the chance to actually put hands on each dog and feel his or her structure. The judge is able to confirm factors in the breed standard such as the dog's angulation, how round the head is, and the size of bone, all features that may not be visible as the dog gaits around the ring.

To begin to teach your Pug to stand on the table, he must first be comfortable being in an elevated position. You can purchase a grooming table for this use or sim-

ply place a rubber bath mat on top of a counter. At first you will want to reward him simply for standing or sitting on the surface. Feeding a meal on the table is a great way for him to associate the elevated surface with a pleasant experience. You can begin to reward him for standing on the surface once he has become comfortable with sitting on it. When he becomes comfortable standing on the table on his own, it is time to teach him how to be hand stacked and then examined.

Home Schooling

Hand Stacking a Pug

You must learn to hand stack in a smooth and quick manner. The goal is to present the prettiest picture for the judge in a short time. First impressions, whether on the floor or on the table, may be the key to whether your Pug wins or loses at a show. Follow these steps whenever you hand stack.

1. Think of hand stacking as a four-step process that goes like this: left front leg, right front leg, left rear leg, right rear leg. You want to set each leg quickly with the entire process taking less than ten seconds.

2. When setting the front legs, use either the shoulder or the elbow. Pick the leg straight up and set it down under the body. Do not try to set the front legs by picking up the feet or the pastern.

3. When setting the rear legs, use the knee to extend the leg so that the hock is perpendicular to the table. Do not

try to set the rear in place by moving his feet.

4. Make sure that the lead is under the chin and that the head is held high. Try to get his attention by letting him nibble on the treat and then pull it away so he leans slightly forward.

5. You will need to learn to be comfortable switching the lead from your left hand into your right hand when you want to set up the left legs, and then back to your left hand to set up the right legs. You will switch the lead back to your left hand when you draw attention forward.

6. Your body position during the table presentation is very important. You do not want to obscure the judge's view. If the judge is looking at your Pug's profile stand in front of him. As the judge approaches from the front move to the dog's side.

7. When hand stacking on the ground, you do not need to move from the front to the side as long as you can lean away. Remember you want to provide an unobstructed view of your Pug at all times.

Once your Pug has learned to stand still on the table it is time to add the examination to the table routine. Have a friend or family member pretend to be the judge. He or she should run hands over your Pug's back as you reward him for standing still. He can nibble on the treat at first but many judges do not want the dog eating during the examination. Ask your helper to touch the head and ears and then continue on to the back once your Pug has mastered the back

touch. As he gets better, the examination can become more thorough. Conformation class will also help your Pug learn to tolerate the table examination.

Fun Matches

Fun matches are events that are run just like a dog show with the exception of awarding championship points. Most all breed kennel clubs are required to have

Your Pug's breeder can advise you on the correct class in which to enter your dog.

at least one fun match each year. Entering a fun match is a great way to get over being nervous about competing for the first time and they're a wonderful way for puppies to get used to being around other dogs. Your Pug also needs to experience different buildings and surroundings before you start entering him in conformation shows. You can visit the American Kennel Club Web site to find a list of kennel clubs in your area.

Grooming for a Show

Pugs are generally considered a "wash-and-wear" breed. They do not require a lot of grooming prior to the show, but some preparation needs to be considered. First, nails must be trimmed as short as possible. A good bath, given a day or two before the show, is a must! You will want to make the dog's outline look as clean as possible, so invest in a good pair of thinning shears and straight scissors.

The hair on the tail and rear legs should be trimmed to present a good outline. You may need to trim stray hairs on the underside of the neck or belly. A little petroleum jelly on the nose and your Pug is ready to go.

The Big Time

You and your Pug are now ready to try your first conformation show. He must be

Pugs need to experience different surroundings before entering conformation competition.

at least six months of age at the time of the show and you'll need to register at least three weeks before the competition. You must also determine which class to enter.

- **Puppy** class is divided into two age divisions, six to nine months and nine to twelve months.
- **12–18 month** is for dogs between the ages of twelve and eighteen months.
- **American Bred** is available to any dog born in the United States.
- **Novice** is open to any dog that has not won three first place ribbons in the Novice class and does not have any championship points.

- **Bred by Exhibitor** is for dogs bred by, owned by, and shown by the breeder.
- **Open** class is for any dog over six months of age.

You will receive an entry ticket with your Pug's number and a judging program approximately one week before the show. Plan to arrive at least an hour in advance of your ring time so that you and your Pug have a little time to get used to the noises of the show. Pick up your armband at the ring where you are competing ten minutes or so before your scheduled ring time. Take a few deep breaths before your class goes into the ring and remember to have fun!

Junior Showmanship

Junior showmanship is a sport for children within the conformation show. In the conformation ring the judge is evaluating the dog. In the Junior Showmanship ring, the judge is evaluating how well the junior handler exhibits the dog. Junior handlers must be skilled at all of the procedures needed to properly present their dog. To be eligible for Junior Showmanship a child must be at least nine years of age. A junior handler number must be assigned to the child from the American Kennel Club before the entry is made.

Junior showmanship classes are divided according to the age of the child.

- **Junior Class** is for children nine to twelve years of age.
- **Intermediate Class** is for children ages twelve to fourteen.
- **Senior Class** is for children from fifteen years to eighteen years of age.

New junior competitors enter in the Novice division of their age class. They continue to compete in the Novice division until they win three first-place ribbons with at least one other junior competitor in the class. Once a junior has three wins he or she can move up to compete in the Open division.

Junior showmanship competitors are some of the most capable handlers in the conformation ring. They spend a lot of time practicing ring procedure with their dogs and can give most adult handlers a run for their money.

Junior showmanship is a great way for children to learn how to train a Pug.

Children should be encouraged to train their Pugs in any venue that they are interested in. The Pug owners of the future are today's kids. If a child learns the skills necessary to train a dog at an early age, there's a better chance of mastering those skills as an adult. With better communication and training skills they have a much better chance of having dogs that are well-behaved, both now and in the future. Not only will they benefit by having a great Pug companion, the Pugs will enjoy the constant companionship!

Glossary

American Kennel Club The largest dog registry in the United States. The American Kennel Club also licenses kennel clubs, promotes dog events and activities, funds canine health research, and inspects commercial breeders.

Angulation The angle that is created when bones meet at the joints.

Bite inhibition A learned behavior in which a dog reduces or inhibits the amount of pressure applied during a bite, either in play or aggressive responses.

Bribe The use of food, toys, or something of value to persuade a dog to perform a behavior.

Broker A person or persons who buy puppies directly from a breeder for resale to another individual or pet store.

Canine freestyle A dog and handler team performs a choreographed routine that combines obedience commands and dance moves, set to music.

Champion A dog who has won enough points, completing the requirements of the American Kennel Club.

Commercial breeder A person who produces a large number of puppies for resale to brokers or for sale over the Internet.

Conditioned reinforcer A sound or cue that, after being paired with a stimulus that previously reinforced a behavior, becomes a reinforcing stimulus itself.

Confinement training The use of a crate or space to aid in raising a puppy. The use of a designated area to keep a puppy from being destructive or eliminating in the house.

Conformation The structure of a dog as it relates to the breed standard.

Contact zone An area of an obstacle in agility competition, designated by yellow paint that must be touched by a dog negotiating the obstacle.

Correction An action that causes an adjustment of a behavior.

Crate A cage or kennel used during confinement training.

Crowding The movement of a dog into the handler's leg during obedience exercises or while on leash. Bumping or leaning on the handler's leg.

Cue A verbal or physical signal that becomes associated with a specific act or learned behavior.

Dam The mother of a dog.

Distraction An event that causes a loss of focus, usually a noise or movement.

Doggie day care A facility that offers boarding services, usually during the

A patient Pug waits for the *release* command.

day, where dogs are allowed to play and interact with one another.

Double cue Earning a qualifying score in both the Standard class and the Jumpers with Weavers class in the same agility trial, on the same day.

Extinction The decline of a behavior when it is no longer reinforced by a reward.

Fault In Agility or Obedience—a mistake made by the dog such as hitting a jump. In Conformation—a deviation from the breed standard.

Fun match An informal event held to provide additional training.

Gait The movement of a dog.

Handler Any person who takes a dog into a conformation ring, companion animal event, or performance event.

Hand signal A visual gesture used to indicate a specific behavior.

Housebroken The act of learning to eliminate in a specific area or on a specific substrate.

Instinctual Any behavior that is natural or unlearned.

Jackpot reward A large number of food treats given to indicate that a response was correct.

Learned behavior A response or reaction that is performed consistently due to past experiences. Any behavior that a dog has mastered in response to a cue.

Leg A qualifying score in obedience competition.

Lunging Jumping forward or a sudden forward movement while a dog is on leash.

Luring The use of a signal or reward to move a dog from a neutral behavior to a desired behavior or response.

Major A win of three, four, or five points in a conformation event.

Marking Elimination by a dog, most commonly urine, used as a territorial signal to other dogs.

Operant conditioning The use of consequences to modify the occurrence and form of behavior.

Pedigree A dog's ancestral paperwork showing his parents, grandparents, and great-grandparents.

Puppy mill A facility that produces puppies in an unhealthy, dirty environment, often without regard for the temperament or well-being of the sire, dam, and litter.

"Q" A qualifying score in agility competition.

Separation anxiety A fear or apprehension of being left alone, often experienced by dogs that have had multiple homes.

Service dog A dog that performs a task or tasks for a human, such as aiding in hearing, sight, or medical detection.

Shake can A device used to startle or interrupt a behavior, made from a soda can containing pennies, rocks, or metal objects.

Sire The father of a dog.

Socialization class A puppy group that uses play to acclimate the students to puppies of varying sizes and ages.

Standard course time The average time allotted to complete an agility course.

Target training The use of an object to teach a dog how to focus. Teaching a dog to touch or move toward an object in order to receive a reward.

Therapy dog A dog that provides comfort, stimulation, and love to individuals in hospitals, health care facilities, and schools.

United Kennel Club The second oldest, second largest dog registry in the United States.

Victorian Pug A type of Pug depicted in art from the Victorian Era, showing a slightly longer nose, taller leg, and much finer bone.

Withers The highest part of the back at the base of the neck.

An example of a well-proportioned Pug head.

Useful Addresses, Web Sites, and Literature

Books

Breed

Belmonte, Brenda. *The Pug Handbook.* New York: Barron's Educational Series, Inc., 2004.

Maggitti, Phil. *Pugs: Everything About Purchase, Nutrition, Breeding, Behavior and Training.* New York: Barron's Educational Series, Inc., 2000.

Hutchinson, Robert. *For the Love of Pugs.* California: Browntrout Publishers, 1998.

Dog Training

Alston, George and Vanacore, Connie. *The Winning Edge; Show Ring Secrets.* New York: John Wiley and Sons, 1992.

Benjamin, Carol Lee. *Second-Hand Dog: How to Turn Yours into a First Rate Pet.* New Jersey: John Wiley and Sons, 1998.

Bonham, Margaret. *Introduction to Dog Agility.* New York: Barron's Educational Series, Inc., 2000.

Coile, D. Caroline, Ph.D. *Show Me.* New York: Barron's Educational Series, Inc., 1997.

Coughlin, Paddy. *Competitive Obedience.* United Kingdom: Interpet Publishing, 2003.

Ludwig, Gerd. *Sit! Stay! Train Your Dog the Easy Way.* New York: Barron's Educational Series, Inc., 2008.

Miller, Pat and Donaldson, Jean. *The Power of Positive Dog Training.* New Jersey: John Wiley and Sons, 2001.

Schlegl-Kofler, Katharina. *The Complete Dog Training Guide.* New York: Barron's Educational Series, Inc., 2008.

Periodicals

The American Kennel Club Gazette
P.O. Box 1956
Marion, OH 43306
(800) 533-7323

Clean Run
17 Industrial Drive
South Hadley, MA 01075
www.cleanrun.com

Front and Finish
P.O. Box 333
Galesburg, IL 61402-0333
www.frontandfinish.com

Pug Talk
5013 Plover Road
Wisconsin Rapids, WI 54494-9705
www.pugtalk.com

Whole Dog Journal
P.O. Box 420234
Palm Coast, FL 32142-0234
www.whole-dog-journal.com

Organizations

American Kennel Club
5580 Centerview Drive
Raleigh, NC 27606
(919) 816-3600
www.akc.org

Association of Pet Dog Trainers
150 Executive Center Drive, Box 35
Greenville, SC 29615
(800) PET-DOGS
www.apdt.com

Canadian Kennel Club
89 Skyway Avenue, Suite 100
Etobicoke, Ontario M9W 6R4
(416) 675-5511
www.ckc.ca

International Association of
    Canine Professionals
P.O. Box 560156
Montverde, FL 34756-0156
(877) THE-IACP
www.dogpro.org

North American Dog Agility Council
P.O. Box 1206
Colbert, OK 74733
www.nadac.com

Pug Dog Club of America
www.pugs.org

Therapy Dogs International
88 Bartley Road
Flanders, NJ 07836
(973) 252-9800
www.tdi-dog.org

United Kennel Club
100 East Kilgore Road
Kalamazoo, MI 49002
(269) 343-9020
www.ukcdogs.com

United States Dog Agility Association
P.O. Box 850955
Richardson, TX 75085
(972) 487-2200
www.usdaa.com

Index